WALKS IN GERTRUDE STEIN'S PARIS

WALKS IN GERTRUDE STEIN'S PARIS

MARY ELLEN JORDAN HAIGHT

GIBBS·SMITH
P
PUBLISHER

PEREGRINE SMITH BOOKS

SALT LAKE CITY

For Raymond, whose faith,
assistance and company supported
me on each step and for R.L.H. 3,
J.J.H. 1 & 2, and D.R.H.

Design by Formaz
Printed in the United States of America

Cover photo: Sylvia Beach and Stephen Vincent Benét in front of
the Shakespeare and Company Bookshop, 8, rue Dupuytren.
Courtesy of Princeton University Library, Sylvia
Beach Collection.

Cataloging-in-Publication Data

Haight, Mary Ellen Jordan.

Walks in Gertrude Stein's Paris
"A Peregrine Smith Book."
Bibliography: p.142 Includes indexes. 1. Stein, Gertrude,
1874-1946—Homes and haunts—France—Paris—Guide-books. 2.
Literary landmarks—France—Paris—Guide-books. 3. Bohemianism—
France—Paris—Guide-books. 4. Walking—France—Paris—
Guide-book. 5. Paris (France)—Description—1975— —Guide-books.
6. Paris (France)—Intellectual life—20th century. I. Title.

PS3537.T323Z644 1988 818'.5209 [B] 87-32731
ISBN 0-87905-268-6

CONTENTS

*Gertrude Stein and Alice B. Toklas. Courtesy of Research Library,
Department of Special Collections, University of California—
Los Angeles.*

HOW TO USE THIS BOOK

This book offers five half-day walking tours of the Left Bank, but it contains much more than maps and landmarks. Read it before you begin a tour to get a sense both of the era and the abundance of artists, thinkers, and celebrities of the Left Bank's heyday, from 1900 to 1940, and see how easily—and often—the paths of genius crossed in Bohemian Paris.

The section of Paris covered in *Walks in Gertrude Stein's Paris* is exclusive to the Left Bank and includes five important museums. Walks I and III begin at the "rag and bone shop of the heart"—just look for the wood likeness of William Shakespeare hanging in front. Like the original bookstore, Shakespeare and Company is a mecca for literary English-speaking residents and tourists alike. Walks I and II, I and III, IV and V, and III and V can be merged together if you are a hearty walker. It is suggested that you review the route before setting out, then keep the map handy while walking. Some may have difficulty walking, reading, and looking at the same time.

Since the *Rive Gauche* is best experienced by wandering along its glamorous boulevards and enjoying its cafés, each walking tour includes a stop where you can rest and order a *café crème* (only before noon) or a demi-tasse of strong expresso, and find yourself suffused in the ambiance of the past.

Although the tours are planned so that the tourist, or *boulevardier,* can complete a walk in about two hours, do allow at least twice that time for your promenade. So many streets—and side streets—offer diversions. If you begin these walks in the morning, you may find certain city blocks filled with vendors; in the afternoon, window displays and inviting cafés may attract; in the evening, street musicians may invite a detour or two. Be sure to allow plenty of time for museums, especially if it is your first visit. A garden such as Rodin's may add hours to your schedule.

To quote Hemingway: "If you are lucky enough to have lived in Paris . . . then wherever you go for the rest of your life it stays with you, like a moveable feast."

ACKNOWLEDGEMENTS

Sara Bernhardt said that San Francisco was the city that next to Paris was the darling of her heart. After San Francisco, Paris is next in my heart. My explorations on foot began in the city by the Golden Gate. The inspiration for many of my wanderings came from Margo Patterson Doss, author of *San Francisco at Your Feet* and a column in the San Francisco *Chronicle*.

I gratefully acknowledge the assistance of many generous people in writing this book. My first-rate assistant, mapper and companion walker was my husband who braved a very cold European winter so I could research the manuscript.

For research sources and materials, James W. Davis, Rare Book Librarian, Department of Special Collections, Library of the University of California at Los Angeles; Brenda Lockwood, Librarian, Bitburg American High School, West Germany; George Whitman, Shakespeare and Company, Paris; Virginia Padover, San Francisco.

For special illustrations, Gisèle Freund and Gregory Lawrance.

For reading the manuscript, Celine Passage, Fulton W. Haight and Sandra Lundgren.

For her inspiration as a teacher of literature, Lynn Snyder.

For his faith in the project, Gibbs M. Smith.

For her patience, knowledge, and enthusiasm in editing the book, Mona Letourneau.

For the motivation they provided with the question, "When is your book going to be published?" my friends in Kyllburg, West Germany, Paris and America.

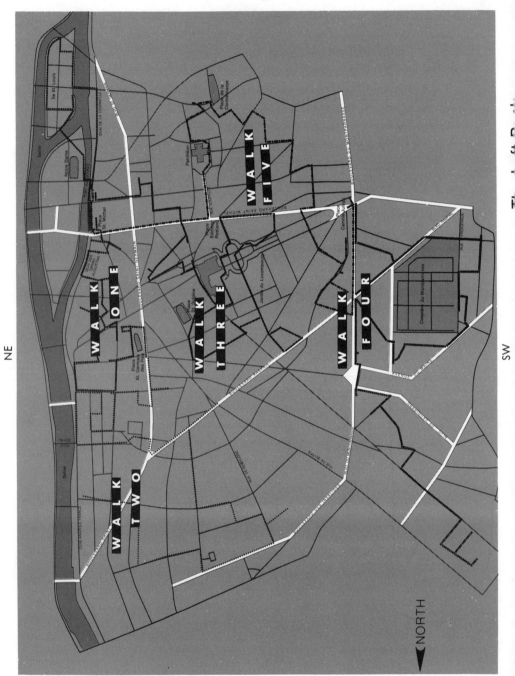

THE LEFT BANK SETTING

For the first forty years of the twentieth century, Paris was the creative center of Western literature and the fine arts. The City of Light, with her broad, tree-lined boulevards and romantic Seine river dividing the cosmopolis into the Left and Right Banks, lured scores of creative, adventurous Americans who were dissatisfied with the homogenous atmosphere of industrial United States. The early expatriates were drawn to the older, more sophisticated French culture, now ending its *Belle-Epoque,* or Golden Age. The physical beauty of Paris, as well as its ambiance, an inspiring admixture of *joie de vivre* and existential courage, nourished artistic experimentation. These forward-looking, post-romantic artists were known as the *avant-garde.*

The Left Bank's cultural notoriety began in the late nineteenth century, when the French modernists of the *avant-garde,* because of the increased development of the Right Bank slopes of Montmartre, migrated across the Seine to the Left Bank Latin Quarter and Montparnasse. The small family farms and vineyards that had graced the Montmartre landscape also disappeared, so that the migration to the Left Bank was a sign that the nineteenth century was indeed ending. New American *emigrés* who arrived here with regular incomes or annuities occupied elegant apartments in the seventeenth and eighteenth century *hôtel-particuliers* of the sixth and seventh *arrondissements.* Others less financially secure lived in small, unsanitary studios in the fifth and sixth arrondissements.

In the preface to Jean Rhys's collection of short stories, *The Left Bank,* Ford Madox Ford observed that the Left Bank of Paris represented the psychological and intellectual opposite of the Right Bank. *Rive Gauche* symbolized all the left banks of the world; it was marginal society's own capitol.

Most of the pre-World War I American expatriates who came to France were alienated in their own comparatively narrow culture which, in many ways, still preferred the conformity and dullness of the Victorian Era. Writers, artists, architects, musicians, decorators, dancers, playwrights and fashion designers came to Paris to abandon tradition and produce unusual, often scandalous, productions. The earlier wave of American-born bohemians were drawn like pilgrims to the shrine of Paris, and many settled here for a lifetime. In comparison with their homelands, Paris seemed tolerant of any extreme of experience.

When Gertrude Stein arrived in Paris in 1903 to share an apartment with her brother Leo, she had already decided to devote her future to scholarly reading and writing. She had found the study of medicine boring, and left John Hopkins University medical school before graduation. Soon after establishing their ménage, the Steins decorated the walls of their atelier with works by modernists such as Henri Matisse, Paul Cézanne, Georges Braque, and Pablo Picasso. Numerous artists were invited to Saturday evening salons at which they mingled with wealthy art patrons, tourists, struggling American writers and artists, eccentrics, and European nobility. This eclectic society was drawn by strong art and Gertrude Stein's imposing figure and notoriety. Not every guest appreciated the Steins' tastes. In 1908 the American painter Mary Cassatt, upon viewing the walls covered with *avant-garde* works, exclaimed, "I have never in my life seen so many dreadful paintings in one place. I have never seen so many dreadful people gathered together and I want to be taken home at once."

Stein embraced the artistic form of cubism which was represented visually in the works of her good friend Picasso. "I was alone at this time in understanding him, perhaps because I was expressing the same thing in literature," wrote Stein. To some moderns her works continue to be repetitive and nonsensical and it is her autobiography, primarily, which she attributed to her life-time companion, Alice Babette Toklas, that granted her recognition and economic independence. *The Autobiography of Alice B. Toklas* is much more popular than Stein's other writing and remains one of the outstanding memoirs in American literature.

"I have a country—America is my country, but Paris is my home town," remarked Stein. To the young Americans, she represented the freedom and creativity they were seeking in Paris. To the French she is still recognized as the true American expatriate whose work and influence thrived in France.

Many other post-war high modernists felt the same desire for independence in the arts, but really were refugees, rather than voluntary exiles, from the American qualities they carried with them. Most were poor, and had seen "Paree" for the first time because of the war. To writers Ernest Hemingway, John Dos Passos and e.e. cummings, Paris was artistically the most alive city in the world. Living was cheap and they could mingle with other Americans in the cafés. Paris was also important because of the now famous Gertrude Stein, and the expatriates of the twenties would often request invitations to her soirées.

After World War I, Europeans referred to young men from the age of eighteen to twenty-five as "the lost generation," *une génération perdue*, because they had missed the period in life when the individual assimilates his culture, or becomes civilized. Compared to the youth of past generations, these young war veterans were aimless, restless, and lacking in purpose. While repairing Gertrude Stein's car, a garageman in Belley, France, described his incompetent young assistant as a member of this lost generation. Stein later repeated the phrase to Ernest Hemingway, who used it in the epigraph of *The Sun Also Rises*. In the novel, Lady Brett Ashley characterizes the personality structure of the lost generation as self-defeating but projects this feeling onto her friends. The term was used widely to signify not only the young European and American veterans who stayed on or returned to Europe, but also to describe the hordes of Americans living and traveling abroad in the twenties whose lack of economic security and responsibility was seen as self-defeating. Members of this crowd who were not serious writers or artists refused to admit to the futility of their lives, and attempted instead to give the illusion of being in control, simply by calling themselves members of a new social calling: the bohemian experience of Paris. Paris was the last frontier for many of them. They sought refuge in the belief that their self-absorption, like self-expression or creativity, was an aesthetically pure expression. Similarly in literature, the internal, private world of the high modernist was explored prolifically through the use of experimental language and literary forms. Works of art, theater, photography, and music focused on the value of art as it was meant for the creator, not the observer. Sigmund Freud's studies of the unconscious and dream analysis suddenly became popular ideas, and further legitimized the subject of personal, inner experience as material for modern art.

When the poet Hart Crane arrived in Paris in 1921, he wrote to a friend, "Paris is really a test for an American. Dinners, soirées, poets, erratic millionaires, painters, translations, lobsters, absinthe, music, promenades, oysters, sherry, aspirins, pictures, sapphic heiresses, editors, books, sailors. And how!"

Three years later, Crane, whose grandfather invented Life Savers, jumped from a ship off the coast of Florida and drowned himself. Joseph Conrad wrote that Crane "had no surface, he was all interior."

In 1919, another American who stayed for her lifetime, Sylvia Beach, the daughter of a Presbyterian minister in Princeton, New Jersey, opened an English language bookstore and lending library called Shakespeare and Company. She intended to promote the literary heritage as well as French contemporary writers. Shakespeare and Company quickly became significant as a club for intellectuals, writers, artists and the *cognoscenti* at large. Wrote Beach, in an unfinished novel dated 1934:

". . . there followed a thin stream of transient maniacs and such few people of real talent as existed at the time on our globe. These would disappear into a back room and give to the shop that atmosphere of a place where things happened which stimulated and excited all who went there. The polished silhouette of Joyce, the swarthy face and broad shoulders of Hemingway, the beard of Fargue, Gide in his cape, Sherwood Anderson—it was a place where people who existed, lived, and people who lived, enjoyed themselves."

In 1926, the exchange rate of the dollar reached a high of fifty francs. The resulting American stock market crash in 1929 was followed by a world-wide economic crash and depression. The literature and art of the thirties reflects this socio-economic crisis with an increase in social and political themes, and the return to narratives full of integrity and strong ethics. Meanwhile, established artists became politically active. Ezra Pound left Paris for Italy and supported the fascists; Pablo Picasso took issue with the rise of fascism in his native Spain; André Gide converted to French communism, Céline became a fascist and disappeared to Africa, and Gertrude Stein discovered democracy in America.

In 1926 Shakespeare and Company became the headquarters of the Walt Whitman Committee of Paris, formed to help the new Walt Whitman Committee of the Authors Club of New York raise funds for a monument to be erected in New York's Battery Park. Sculptor Jo Davidson, Beach's good friend, designed the project. Beach owned several rough-drafts by Whitman, and the fund-raising event held in the shop on April 20 exhibited manuscripts, original editions, photographs, and drawings by Whitman. The monument in New York was never erected, but no doubt Whitman's work was now better known in France.

Whitman was a major international influence on modern authors. Valery Larbaud was eighteen years old when he

James Joyce and Sylvia Beach—reading Ulysses. *Courtesy of the Princeton University Library, Sylvia Beach Collection.*

discovered the writings of Whitman, and in his homage to *"Paris de France,"* he wrote:

> *". . . that does not prevent us from fraternally welcoming the Parisians from outside France, that is to say, foreigners who have been and are able to contribute to the material activity of Paris and to its spiritual power, like Walt Whitman.*

To which Whitman replied, "I am a real Parisian."

In the late modernist period of the thirties the Americans who lived in Paris on small proceeds from their work, investments, or family loans and gifts were gradually driven home by the drop in value of the dollar. Those who were successful or well off stayed on through the decade, but, in 1940, with the fall of Paris to the Nazis, the glorious years of this modern age ended. The brilliant city, *La Ville de Lumière* was dimmed.

WALK ONE

THE LITERARY QUARTER

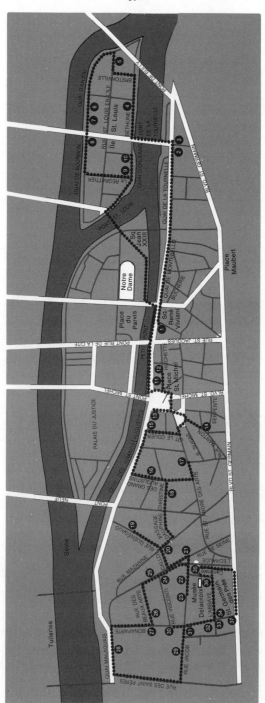

WALK I

Métro St.-Michel; Buses 24, 27, 47, 63, 86, 87

If you begin this walk by arriving at the Place St.-Michel via the Métro bus, then find the southwest corner of the Quai St.-Michel through the crowds of people always found on the sidewalks here. Commence walking south along the quai, keeping the view of Notre Dame across the Seine in front of you. After one block, cross Rue St.-Jacques to the small Square Mariette, one of two green open spaces still in existence on the banks of the river. On the far side of the square, where in warm weather local residents play *boules,* and to the right, is the short, picturesque Rue de la Bûcherie.

1. Shakespeare and Company
37, rue de la Bûcherie

Start south from Shakespeare and Company along the Quai de Montebello following a route much travelled in the twenties and thirties by writers and artists fortunate enough to live and work in this unique corner of Paris. There were fewer motorized vehicles then, considerably less urban noise and many more anglers casting their lines in the Seine. The elderly trees are taller and the cobblestones are a bit more worn. Fluffs of clouds and the cerulean sky still draw one's attention upwards to the jagged, majestic spires of Notre Dame. It's easy to return to past scenes of Paris because it is a city that does not change.

On the right as you pass Square Viviani, look for a false acacia reputed to be the oldest tree in Paris. It is next to the Church of St. Julien-le-Pauvre, the oldest church in Paris (twelfth century). The tree is propped up on cement supports, but it still blooms every spring. With Notre Dame Cathedral on your left, stop at the first building past the old Public Assistance Hospital of Paris, now called the Musée de L'Assistance Publique.

Continue down Quai de la Tournelle toward Pont de la Tournelle. Near the right corner are two interesting landmarks.

2. Residence of John Dos Passos and John Howard Lawson
45, quai de la Tournelle

After the first World War, American servicemen willing to postpone their return to the United States were allowed to study at European schools. In the spring of 1919, after being discharged from the American Ambulance Corps, the American novelist and poet, John Dos Passos, attended classes in anthropology at the University of Paris, Sorbonne. While sharing the apartment here, he wrote,

> *". . . . I feel like jumping in the Seine. . . . At any moment I expect . . . the roof of the house to open like the corolla of a flower, or the gutters of the Quai de la Tournelle to run amethysts . . . and all this is caused by six fine days and the prospect of demobilization."*

Dos Passos began *Three Soldiers* (1921), a novel based on his recent war experiences, then left Paris to become a roving foreign correspondent reporting on the Peace Conference at Versailles. After climbing in the Pyrenees with his friend, fellow American author e.e. cummings, in the spring of 1921, he returned to the apartment to complete *Rosinante to the Road Again* (1922).

The permanent resident of the apartment was Dos Passos' friend and landlord, playwright John (Jack) Howard Lawson. About their life together Dos Passos wrote, "We ate well and drank well and loaned each other money when we ran out . . . . We led a fine life." Lawson was writing the play *Roger Bloomer* at the time. He became a Hollywood screenwriter in the thirties, and in the forties when Senator Joseph McCarthy accused the entertainment industry of harboring communists, Lawson was named as one of the infamous "Hollywood Ten."

Cross Rue du Cardinal-Lemoine to the south corner.

3. La Tour d'Argent
Pont de la Tournelle and Quai de la Tournelle

In the twenties, this restaurant let a few rooms and gave the boarders a discount on food. Books left behind by the renters were sold by the *valet de chambre* for a few francs to the proprietor of a book stall on the quai. She disdained books written in English and sold them cheaply to Ernest Hemingway.

Go east across the Pont de la Tournelle, with the renowned picture of the flying buttresses of Notre Dame on your left, and proceed to the most expensive piece of real estate in the city. Today it is home to the affluent but in the early part of the century writers and publishers enjoyed the quiet, narrow streets. One could live here among the tiny shops and restaurants and never need to leave the island for the surrounding noisy boulevards. Behind the forbidding tall walls penetrated only through massive doors are 300 to 400-year-old *hôtel-particuliers*. Most are divided into stately apartments, one or two to a floor, around a central courtyard.

After crossing the bridge, turn immediately right and walk along the Seine for one block. The next landmark will be on your left.

4. Residence of Helena Rubenstein
24 , quai de Béthune

When, in 1930, cosmetic tycoon Helena Rubenstein purchased the beautiful private house here overlooking the Seine, she had to wait five years to evict the French tenants. The building, similar in design to those adjoining, was demolished and then replaced by this art-deco model designed by Louis Sue. Notice the elaborately carved wooden doors from the old house. The simplicity of the design and the bulk of the stone front declare a separateness from its traditional genteel French neighbors. I was once standing on the quai when a resident slipped through the entry doors, providing me a quick look at the large court with green plants surrounding a fountain topped by a Greek statue.

While dividing her time between this penthouse and New York, Rubenstein was separated from bookseller and publisher Edward Titus. In one of the most affluent residences in Paris, Rubenstein collected works by the modernists. She bought in bulk because she believed art to be a tangible investment. The Rubenstein collection included the works of Marc Chagall, Georges Braque, Pablo Picasso, Amedeo Modigliani and Georges Rouault.

In mid-May of 1940, with the German army driving toward Paris through the Marne valley, the booming of giant cannons could be heard by refugees fleeing the city. With her husband Prince Artchil Gourielli-Tchkonia of Georgia, the princess hurriedly sailed for New York, leaving behind priceless art and antiques. During the next four years, German military occupied the rooms, which were found after the Armistice to be looted and extensively damaged.

Stand across the street on the quai and look for the roof garden. It contained fountains, flowerbeds, perennial green plants and a Greek statuary.

Continue to the next corner on the quai, at Rue de Bretonville, and turn left; at the end of the block after passing under a building which extends over the narrow street, turn right onto

Ile St.-Louis in the Thirties. Courtesy of Gisèle Freund

Quai des Grand-Augustins in the twenties, a view from the Murphys' apartment. Photo credit: Honoria Murphy Donnelly, courtesy of Holt, Rhinehart and Winston.

Rue St.-Louis-en-l'Ile. Across from the mansion lived in by the Baron Guy de Rothschild and his wife Marie-Hélène, on the "Main Street" of this exclusive island, is an old building with white shutters.

5. Residence of William Aspenwall Bradley
5, rue St.-Louis-en-l'Ile

Writer and editor William Aspenwall Bradley, who worked in Paris as a literary agent for Harcourt, Brace, settled here with his French wife. In her *New Yorker* column, "Letter from Paris," Genet (Janet Flanner) called him "the leading agent and prophet here on transatlantic matters."

A noted literary source to expatriate Americans on this side of the Atlantic, Bradley had many important clients including Katherine Anne Porter, Natalie Clifford Barney, Ezra Pound, Edith Wharton, John Dos Passos, Stephen Vincent Benét, William Shirer and Thornton Wilder. After writing *The Autobiography of Alice B. Toklas* in six weeks, Gertrude Stein submitted the manuscript to Bradley. By return mail he stated: "I have forwarded your manuscript to Harcourt, Brace. Congratulations—it's a sure hit!"

Take a left at the Seine, following the high wall that surrounds the Rothschilds' garden, along the quai to a rust-colored door.

6. Former Offices of the *Transatlantic Review* and Three Mountains Press
29, quai d'Anjou

Located in what was an ancient wine cellar were the offices of Ford Madox Ford, novelist and editor of *Transatlantic Review*. Like Gertrude Stein's atelier or Sylvia Beach's Shakespeare and Company, it was one of the places in Paris where the renaissance of English prose began. Ford, author of *It Was the Nightingale* and *The Good Soldier,* worked in a cagelike office beneath a vaulted ceiling.

It was fortunate that the office held only a single occupant because Ernest Hemingway, the unpaid assistant editor, and Ford had a strained relationship. The eccentric Ford had a snobbish demeanor and Hemingway found him physically repellant. Although he liked the way Ford edited the magazine, he disagreed with Ford's policy and taste. The magazine printed too many conventional and surrealist works; Hemingway wanted to publish the works of Americans he admired. In pleasant weather, Hemingway would escape the office to read manuscripts outside on the lower ramp of the quai. On wet days he worked inside at the nearby Rendezvous des Mariniers.

While Ford was in America raising funds for the review, Hemingway serialized Gertrude Stein's lengthy novel, *The Making of Americans.* At this time, Stein and Hemingway were close friends and Stein served as his mentor, but she was having trouble finding publishers for her works. Ford at first agreed to pay Stein by the page. After four installments, however, Ford claimed that Hemingway had misrepresented the great length of the piece, and that Stein should have been paid a lump sum.

At his Thursday afternoon teas, Ford offered delicacies prepared by his paramour, Stella Bowen, the mother of his daughter, Julia. Gertrude Stein and Alice B. Toklas would often stop by for tea and be greeted by the portly Ford whose face, adorned by a long drooping moustache, reminded Ernest Hemingway of a golden walrus.

The wine cellar was also home to William Bird's Three Mountains Press. Named for Mont Sainte-Geneviève, Montparnasse and Montmartre, the small company produced outstanding books printed on fine paper. Ezra Pound edited Ford's *Women and Men, The Great American Novel,* by poet William Carlos Williams, and *In Our Time* by Hemingway.

When Robert McAlmon moved the Contact Publishing Company from his room on the Rue de l'Odéon, in 1924, he and Bird joined for two years in distributing the works of both firms.

From 1922 to 1925, Hemingway sometimes went into the Three Mountains at night to set his latest work in type. Then he would make proofs of the pages on Bird's seventeenth-century handpress, to see how the story appeared in print.

7. Residence of John Dos Passos
37, quai d'Anjou

Returning from the peace conference of 1920 where he worked as a roving reporter, John Dos Passos lived here for a short time in an upstairs apartment. While writing *Manhattan Transfer* in 1922, Dos Passos met James Joyce at Shakespeare and Company. "I shook the limp hand of a pale uninterested man in dark glasses sitting beside the stove in the back room." Upon reading *Ulysses* for the first time, Dos Passos noted that its publication "disposed of the current theory that the English novel is dead."

Continue past Pont Marie. The street name changes to the Quai de Bourbon. Stop at the restaurant in the third building from the corner.

8. Formerly Le Rendezvous des Mariniers
7, quai de Bourbon

The Rendezvous des Mariniers, managed by Madame Le Conte, served good, simple food. While waiting in Paris in 1917 for assignment in Italy as a Red Cross ambulance driver, Dos Passos stayed in a room above the restaurant and almost became a Le Conte family member. Unlike most of the Americans living in Paris, Dos Passos would speak French and socialize with the Parisians. His amiability, as well as his lively interest in French literature, endeared him to the Le Contes.

In Hemingway's novel, *The Sun Also Rises,* characters Jake Barnes and Bill Gorton come here to eat a meal of roast chicken, new green beans, mashed potatoes, salad and apple pie and cheese. Then they walk around the island to Quai d'Orléans, Quai Béthune, cross Pont de la Tournelle on what was then a wooden foot bridge, and walk up the steep Rue du Cardinal-Lemoine to Place de la Contrescape.

Follow the quai northwest and turn onto Rue le Regrattier. The next landmark will be on your left, on the south side of the street.

9. Residence of Nancy Cunard
2, rue le Regrattier

On the corner of this narrow street and the Quai d'Orléans is the east-facing apartment once occupied by English shipping heiress, Nancy Cunard. Poet William Carlos Williams described Cunard, the prototype flapper, as "straight as a stick, emaciated, holding her head erect, not particularly animated, her blue eyes untroubled, inviable in her virginity of pure act."

Nancy Cunard's first collection of poems was published in 1921, but it was her lifestyle, rather than her writing, that made her famous. In Michael Arlen's novel, *The Green Hat,* Cunard is portrayed as the character Iris. Inherited wealth made it possible for Cunard to be flamboyant in her support of talented artists, particularly toward the surrealists often seen at her daily salons at 5 P.M. Louis Aragon, an author and founder of the surrealist movement, was her frequent companion and close friend.

The large rooms of the apartment were decorated in Afrosurrealist mode with paintings by Giorgio de Chirico, Francis Picabia, and Yves Tanguy hanging beside African tribal masks. Black and white tiles covered the floors and in the main room sat a leopard skin couch and a stunning boulevard desk that had belonged to her father, English shipping magnate Sir Bache Cunard.

Walk southeast again along the quai one block.

10. Residence of Harry and Caresse Crosby
12, quai d'Orléans

In the summer of 1923 playboy-banker Harry Crosby and his wife Caresse, *née* Mary (Polly) Phelps Jacob Peabody, had a rowboat which they would tie to a willow tree along the quai, across from their small-balconied windows overlooking the Seine. The red boat served as Crosby's transportation to work at the French branch of Morgan Guaranty Trust Company

Caresse, in a bathing suit, and Harry, in a proper banker's suit, would row downstream to the Quai des Tuileries. While Caresse rowed back up the river, Harry would walk through the Jardin des Tuileries to Number 14, Place Vendôme, opposite the Ritz Hotel. How convenient for the bored nephew of J. P. Morgan to leisurely lunch at the Ritz bar.

As a debutante in New York City, Polly Jacob had invented the wireless brassiere, later selling the patent to the Warner Brothers Corset Company.

Caresse wrote that she "loved to go marketing in the twisty back streets of the tiny island." But the apartment's rooms were too small for two children and the servants. Harry couldn't bear the noise made by the boy and girl from her previous marriage to Richard Peabody of Boston, so the family moved in the autumn.

In December, Crosby resigned his position at Morgan/Harjes; banking didn't run in his blood the way lavish life did. He preferred the company of aesthetes. The couple composed love poems to each other and later established their Black Sun Press, initially to publish their own writings.

Backtrack on the tree-lined quai and turn left onto the short Pont St.-Louis. Cross to the Ile de la Cité, stroll through the Square Jean XXIII behind the cathedral to Pont au Double, and cross over to the Left Bank. Continue west along Quai de Montebello, which becomes Quai St.-Michel at this point. Ernest Hemingway described what it was like to walk along these quais when he finished work or was trying to think something out:

> *It was easier to think if I was walking and doing something or seeing people doing something they understood. At the Head of the Ile de la Cité below the Point Neuf . . . the island ended in a point like the sharp bow of a ship and there was a small park at the edge with fine chestnut trees, huge and spreading, and in the currents and backwaters that the Seine made flowing past, there were excellent places to fish.*

11. Residence of Henri Matisse
27, quai St.-Michel

Although extremely poor at the time they met Gertrude Stein in 1905, Henri and Adelie Matisse enjoyed an exciting view of the Seine and Notre Dame from their small, top-floor, three-room apartment. Mme. Matisse operated a millinery shop on Rue de Chateaudun and their two sons, Jean and Pierre, stayed with grandparents. The Matisses lived like typical middle-class Frenchmen, unlike other artists living in the Latin Quarter. She was a good cook and an immaculate housekeeper; he was a serious person, always conservatively dressed. When painting large canvases such as the "Bonheur de Vivre," Matisse worked in a separate studio.

Gertrude and Leo Stein admired his painting, "Femme au Chapeau" (Woman With the Hat) on display at the 1905 Salon d'Automne. For five hundred francs ($100) they purchased the portrait. The artist's wife wears a grand black hat, the somberness of the black relieved by slashes of orange and green. Controversy about modern art in general was raised by the work when it was shown at the Salon. In 1915 the painting was sold to the Steins' brother Michael, and then in 1950 to Mr. and Mrs. Walter Haas of San Francisco for $20,000. Many of the paintings originally collected by the Steins now belong to the San Francisco Museum of Modern Art.

With the Steins' patronage and their subsequent purchase of his work, the fortunes of the Matisse family improved. By 1909, galleries were buying the colorful yield of Matisse's disciplined, long work sessions. Gertrude Stein was now favoring Pablo Picasso, but Michael and Sarah Stein continued to be close friends with the Matisse family.

Turn left at the St.-Michel Métro stop and left again between the bookstalls at Rue de la Huchette. Notice the width of the street. Walk east to where the street narrows in front of the hotel. Baron Georges-Eugene Haussmann, city planner for Napoleon III, widened the Blvd. St.-Michel end of the street. That is the reason why the buildings from Blvd. St.-Michel to the recently remodeled hotel are nineteenth century in contrast to the twelfth century edifices typifying the old Rue de la Huchette just beyond.

12. Formerly Hôtel du Caveau
28, rue de la Huchette

Newspaperman Elliot Paul settled in the Hôtel du Caveau after World War I. He was then writing the column, "From a Litterateur's Notebook," for the European edition of New York's *Herald Tribune.* He later became the literary editor and city editor of the *Chicago Tribune, European Edition.* While here living in a back room, Paul associated with the residents of the Latin Quarter, recalling his personal account of life there in 1925 in *The Last Time I Saw Paris* (1942).

Elliot Paul was another American who spoke fluent French, mingled with the people and had a passionate desire to know and understand them. On his accordion he learned to play "Trail of the Lonesome Pine," Gertrude Stein's favorite song. With violin accompaniment by Bravig Imbs, they played while Stein sang, *"My name is June and very, very soon . . ."*

Go back to Place St.-Michel, turn left and cross the very busy intersection.

13. Formerly Café St.-Michel, formerly Café de la Gare
Place St.-Michel and Quai des Grands-Augustins

In the heart of the student quarter of the nearby Sorbonne are the many cafés of Place St.-Michel. The corner café was a favorite of Ernest Hemingway. He described it as "a pleasant café, warm and clean and friendly." Dining on the second floor with Morley Callaghan, Ernest and Hadley Hemingway admired the view of Ile de la Cité and Notre Dame.

Next door was the Café de la Gare, which provided Samuel Putnam with

". . . a good place from which to view the life of the student quarter in the morning . . . when the polyglot throng came trooping in for a coffee and crescent before going to classes.

As the square outside rapidly filled with buses and trams and human beings and the chestnut-vendor and the woman selling papers cried their wares, one might listen to an animated argument at a nearby table."

In *Paris Was Our Mistress* (1947), Putnam describes starting a few blocks northwest on Rue de l'Odéon, then walking east to Blvd. St.-Germain, turning left towards Place St.-Germain, crossing the street to the Café aux Deux Magots, the Café de Flore, turning down Rue Bonaparte to the Seine, and following the river back south in the general direction of Notre Dame to the Place St.-Michel, as a scenic route for his morning coffee.

As for our present walk, turn away from the Seine, walk through Place St.-André-des-Arts and turn right on Rue Danton.

14. Residence of Isadora Duncan
5, rue Danton

One Paris designer attributed modern women's freedom from stays and corsets to Isadora Duncan. Duncan was the first dancer to appear in public ungirdled, barefoot and free. Wrote fellow-expatriate Edith Wharton, "Suddenly I beheld the dance I had always dreamed of, a flaming of movement into movement and endless interweaving of emotion and movement. . . . All through the immense rapt audience one felt the rush of her inspiration." Dancing with unstructured, flowing movements, based on ancient Greek dances, and dressed in light sheer toga-like robes, Duncan appeared in theaters all over Europe and America.

In 1909, Duncan rented two large flats here. She lived in the ground floor rear and on the first floor above conducted her school of dance.

While following her around Europe, Auguste Rodin sketched thousands of drawings of her lovely figure. Many of the drawings now hang in the Musée Rodin. The bas-reliefs on the Théâtre des Champs-Elysées, sculpted by Antoine Bourdelle, are based on the figure of Duncan.

When sewing machine heir Paris Singer wished to build Duncan a theater near the Champs-Elysées, they discussed the plans with Louis Sue, architect for Helena Rubenstein. Singer was the father of one of Duncan's two children who had died young in a tragic accident. She mourned their loss until her own accidental death in 1927.

Turn back down Rue Danton to Place St.-André-des-Arts, and walk up Rue St.-André-des-Arts. Turn right onto Rue Gît-le-Coeur and go right. Follow this street back to the Seine. You will pass the Ecole César Franck on your left, and the former Hotel Gît-le-Coeur, home to American beat poets in the fifties, on your right. The next landmark is at the corner of Quai des Grands-Augustins.

15. Residence of Gerald and Sara Murphy
23, quai des Grands-Augustins

The old building here with the entrance on Rue Gît-le-Cour was the Paris home of the wealthy and attractive Gerald and Sara Murphy when they moved to France with their daughter and two sons both for cultural nourishment and to escape their prominent families. Gerald Murphy told people they left America because "there was something depressing to young married people about a country that could pass the Eighteenth Amendment. The country was tightening up and it was depressing." According to Sara Murphy, Paris was "like a great fair and everybody was young."

After the Murphys moved to Europe, the elegant top floor apartment was lived in monthly or seasonally because the Murphys spent a majority of their time, when in Europe, in the Villa America at Cap d'Antibes on the French Riviera.

F. Scott Fitzgerald, a member of their circle of friends that also included Hemingway, Archibald MacLeish, John Dos Passos, Robert Benchley, Dorothy Parker, Donald Ogden Stewart, Jean Cocteau and Pablo Picasso, styled the characters Dick and Nicole Diver in *Tender is the Night* (1933) after the Murphys. The book is dedicated to them and the novel was planned by Fitzgerald to be "one in which the leisure class is at their truly most brilliant and glamorous, such as the Murphys." The Murphys were understandably unhappy that their frequent houseguest Fitzgerald revealed certain facts about their personal lives.

Gerald Murphy and Dos Passos painted scenery together during the summer of 1921 for the Ballets Russes. The Murphys, said Dos Passos, "spent their money well and lavishly."

Murphy was a student of the painter Fernand Léger, who adopted cubism, painting in the bright flat colors of posters. His works often depicted twentieth-century technology. Léger suggested to Murphy, who was wealthy, that a painter could live with his work being of little importance, but it was only a life of suffering that produced meaningful paintings.

Murphy, Dos Passos and Fernand Léger once walked along this quai in the twenties, while Léger pointed out its exciting shapes and colors. Wrote Dos Passos of the experience,

> *". . . Instead of the hackneyed and pastel-tinted Tuileries and bridges and barges and bateaux-mouches on the Seine, we were walking through a freshly invented world . . . the banks of the Seine never looked banal again after that walk."*

Continue along the quai for two blocks, then turn left at Rue des Grands-Augustins.

16. Residence of Pablo Picasso
7, rue des Grands-Augustins

Now a successful artist, Pablo Picasso moved to this seventeenth-century *hôtel-particulier,* former home of the Dukes of Savoie, in 1936. He would occupy an apartment on the second floor with a huge studio on the floor above for the following twenty years. The running of the household was directed by factotum Sabartes, while Marcel, another servant, chauffered the limousine.

Picasso frequented the nearby Café de Flore where his dark Spanish presence, even in the teeming restaurant, projected a feeling of power. To Alice B. Toklas, his conversation was "flabbergasting." On matters of money Picasso observed, "I am anti-commercial, but I am interested in money because I know what I want to do with it."

During the Spanish Civil War his personal war against fascism was fought in the paintings he did here. As a loyalist, he decried organized brutality. In 1937 he created a series of etchings, "The Dream and the Lie of France," a violent surrealist poem to go with the plates.

In the same year, Picasso painted his huge mural *Guernica* (eleven feet by nearly twenty-six feet) which he had meant to hang in the Prado Museum in Madrid when freedom and democracy were enjoyed by all Spanish citizens. After dictator Franco's death in 1975, Spain became a republic with King Juan Carlos as titular head. *Guernica* now hangs in a special wing of the Prado.

Gertrude Stein's attempt to define the genius of Picasso—at one time she remarked that there were only three geniuses in the world, herself, Alfred North Whitehead and Picasso—also defines the creative individual:

> ". . . Picasso only sees something else, another reality. Complications are always easy but another vision than that of all the world is very rare. That is why geniuses are rare, to complicate things in a new way that is easy, but to see the things in a new way that is really difficult, everything prevents one, habits, schools, daily life, reason, necessities of daily life, indolence, everything prevents one, in fact there are very few geniuses in the world."

Continue down Rue des Grands-Augustins and turn left into Rue St.-André-des-Arts.

17. Residence of e.e. cummings
46, rue St.-André-des-Arts

> "The Cathedral of Notre Dame does not budge an inch for all the idiocies of this world."—e.e. cummings

In 1923, cummings was a struggling poor artist. In the mornings he shopped on a delightful nearby market street, rue de Buci, for food bargains, painted in the afternoons in his small single room here, and wrote poetry until late in the evening. His modernist poetry explored new literary forms and alternative uses of punctuation. When he lived here, a friend had just purchased cummings' first self-portrait.

Return toward and turn right onto Rue des Grands-Augustins. Take a left onto Rue Christine.

18. Residence of Gertrude Stein and Alice B. Toklas
5, rue Christine

When, in 1938, Gertrude Stein and Alice B. Toklas moved the famous art collection to this seventeenth-century building, the walls of the flat, formerly occupied by Queen Christina of Sweden, still held the queen's *boiseries* (carved wood panels) and her reading cabinet. The new residents' 131 canvases included five unhung Picassos. Ninety-one of the works, including a Cézanne, Picasso's portrait of Stein, his *Full Length Nude, Girl With a Basket of Flowers,* and nineteen smaller pieces, as well as two paintings by Braque, were hung in the salon.

At first Toklas planned to carpet the fine parquet wooden floors to cut down on the noise, but two friends talked her out

*Helena Rubenstein. Courtesy of the International Museum of
Photography at George Eastman House.*

*Nancy Cunard. Courtesy of Princeton University Library, Sylvia
Beach Collection.*

of it by offering to pay for the refinishing of the floors. "A nice English boy" moved Stein's books and the French plumber was unusually prompt and efficient. Toklas no longer had the need to extoll the talents of American plumbers.

After Stein died on July 27, 1946, in the American Hospital in the Parisian suburb of Neuilly, Toklas lived here alone until forced to move in 1964, three years before her death in 1967. The art collection had previously been moved to a Paris bank vault by Allan Stein's widow, to be held for her three children.

Continue west up Rue Christine and cross Rue Dauphine. Go through the large door to the charming Passage Dauphine. Exiting the passage, turn right on Rue Mazarine, and right again at the next block. Walk up Rue Guénégaud to the next landmark.

19. Former Offices of Hours Press
15, rue Guénégaud

Hours Press was founded in 1929 by the English heiress and socialist-poet, Nancy Cunard. She purchased the seventeenth-century handpress from William Bird for three hundred francs. Hours Press was one of the few artistic and financially successful small presses of the period. Among sixteen works published between 1930 and 1932 were *A Draft of the XXX Cantos* by Ezra Pound and *Whoroscope* by Samuel Beckett.

Go back down Rue Guénégaud, cross Rue Mazarine and go to the corner of Rue Jacques-Callot.

20. Formerly Galerie de la Jeune Peinture or Galerie Surréaliste
3, rue Jacques-Callot

This one-block street was the setting on New Year's Eve 1932, of the New Review art show. At the midnight exhibit held here, 32 painters and five sculptors were represented. The exuberant merry-makers spilled outside the small gallery, filling the entire block with people. As gallons of champagne were consumed, the gutters literally flowed with bubbles.

Extreme modernists, such as Joseph Stella, who believed that the galleries were favoring more conservative artists, were also present at the show. The feeling was so strong between the rival groups of artists that it erupted in a brawl of canes and café chairs in the Café du Dôme. The police were called in to break up the fight.

Continue up Jacques-Callot to the corner and then turn left onto Rue de Seine.

21. Residence of Pablo Picasso
57, rue de Seine

When the young Picasso arrived in Paris in 1900 from his native Barcelona, he was homesick, depressed, poor, and often hungry. He made two lengthy visits home, staying here on one return in 1903. This began his Blue Period, about which Gertrude Stein wrote, ". . . he became once more completely Spanish. . . . the Spanish temperament was again very real inside him." In his somber mood, he painted beggars and human derelicts in tones of blue. "The Old Guitarist" emblematizes this period.

In 1904, he settled in Montmartre in a rustic building shared with poet Max Jacobs and painter Georges Braque. They were friendly, protective neighbors. There Picasso painted *Young Girl With a Basket of Flowers,* the first of his canvasses purchased by the Steins.

Now cross the Rue de Seine, pass a tiny square on your right, cross Rue de l'Echaude and continue west onto Rue Jacob.

22. Residence of Natalie Clifford Barney
20, rue Jacob

For sixty years, the ardent feminist Natalie Clifford Barney occupied the seventeenth-century townhouse in the rear of the courtyard. From 1909 until her death in 1973, she stayed in the *pavillon* that is reputed to have once belonged to Louis XIV's mistress, Ninon de Lenclos. To the right of the two-story building, behind metal gates and hidden from view, is the garden containing the small reproduction of a Doric Temple of Friendship (L'Amitié). It was often the setting for elaborate theatrical productions. On one occasion, attended only by women, famed spy Mata Hari was reputed to have belly danced *sans costume.*

A peek through the metal gates in the Rue Jacob courtyard reveals a neatly tended garden. In Barney's day, the garden was described as lovely and rambling. A curtain of ivy hung over the walls, and a huge tree, splendidly spread over the house, grew in the courtyard. The ruins of L'Amitié and the tree growing outside the dining room still stand.

The first floor of the house contains two rooms, a reception room and a dining room with two windows overlooking the garden. The salons were held in the latter, centered by an ample round table loaded with cucumber sandwiches and cakes, especially chocolate. Above the dining room, Barney's bedroom featured an Empire couch, large polar-bear rug, bed, and writing desk beneath shelves of books—all of poetry. The dwelling was furnished in tapestries, mirrors, sofa beds covered in brown velvet and a grand piano.

Oscar Wilde's niece, Dolly Wilde, declared that the house was so "frowzy" and damp that if you turned up the chairs you would find oysters growing over the bottoms. In all the years of her residence, Barney never remodeled or modernized beyond bringing the electricity in from the Rue St.-Germain. This was the first building in the neighborhood to have electricity.

Barney's legendary Friday afternoon salons were often attended by such prominent French and American literary personalities as Paul Valéry, André Gide, Ezra Pound, Sidonie Colette, William Carlos Williams, Virgil Thomson and Sinclair Lewis. On New Year's Day 1925, she sponsored the first performance of George Antheil's experimental *First String Quartet*. It was in June that year that the American composer's *Ballet Mécanique,* played on a mechanical piano, propellers, fans, xylophones and other pieces of twentieth century hardware, was premiered at the Théâtre des Champs-Elysées. The audience included Barney, James Joyce, T. S. Eliot, Sylvia Beach, Adrienne Monnier, Ezra Pound, and Constantin Brancusi in the packed 2500-seat hall. Halfway through the piece a large part of the audience broke out in boos, shrieks and hisses. As fights broke out in the orchestra, an agitated Antheil shouted from the stage, "Get out if you don't like it." By the completion of the piece, most of the disgruntled patrons had fled. The twenty-five-year-old composer considered the performance to be a huge success.

Evenings when the two friends were in Paris, Barney joined Gertrude Stein for a walk with Stein's second large white poodle, "Basket 2."

Walking back through the carriage entrance, note the low-ceilinged rooms above. Barney's faithful maid Berthe lived here with a good view of the courtyard and her employer's visitors.

Alice B. Toklas before portrait of Gertrude Stein by Picasso.
Courtesy of Research Library, Department of Special Collections,
University of California—Los Angeles.

She was emphatic in her denial that she had ever spent a night in Barney's house. The late-night female visitors were not of her proclivity.

After the Second World War, novelist Richard Wright chose to expatriate in Paris. He died in 1960, and his widow later occupied an apartment in the main building.

Turn back to the small Rue de l'Echaude and turn left onto Rue de Seine.

23. Residence of Colette
28, rue Jacob

In depressingly dark third-floor rooms, Gabrielle-Sidonie Colette Willy, a young recent bride from a village in Burgandy, wrote recollections of her school days at the insistence of her husband. In 1900 *Claudine à l'Ecole* was published, signed by her spouse, Henry Gauthier-Villars, better known as Willy. The book sold 40,000 copies in two months. The ruthless Willy thereafter would lock up his wife for many hours each day so that she had no alternative but to write. Wealthy at last from the popularity of the book, Willy and Colette moved to the Right Bank in the following year, and *Claudine à Paris* appeared in 1901. After four *Claudine* stories, Colette published *Dialogues de Bêtes* under her own name. By 1906 her enslavement to Willy ended with their divorce. Her second career as a dancer and mime in the theater was beginning to blossom.

Colette was described as very petite, with a triangular face and a horror of being disturbed. To Paul Claudel, among others, Colette was the greatest living writer in France in the twenties.

Cross the street and continue towards the Seine.

24. Residence of Ezra Pound
Rue de Seine

On this street of art galleries, in the twenties, poet Ezra Pound could be heard loudly practicing his bassoon. Through his friendship with Pound, James Joyce was invited to Barney's salon. Not all of the new acquaintances Joyce made in Paris were impressed by his superior opinion of himself. While Pound was out of town, Joyce wrote to him:

"I heard and saw no more of the many lucky mortals who made my acquaintance here. I suspect that the pleasure my

exhilarating company gave them will last for the rest of their natural existences."

25. Formerly Akademia Raymond Duncan
31, rue de Seine

What a picture Raymond Duncan made dressed in a toga, sandals on his feet and a laurel wreath crowning his hair, lecturing on Greek philosophy and ancient Greece to his disciples at the Akademia Raymond Duncan. At a villa in the suburb of Neuilly, fifteen or so adults and children lived as a commune. The disciples of Duncan wove rugs, painted posters and kept a vegetarian diet. The leather sandals they assembled to be sold as handmade in Duncan's two shops were actually cut by professionals. The garden of the villa held two bathtubs used for the preparation of batiks and the dyeing of scarves. The tubs were stolen from the nearby villa belonging to Duncan's sister, Isadora, in payment of a financial debt he felt she owed him.

Continue north on Rue de Seine and turn left at the first street towards the Seine.

26. Formerly Hôtel D'Alsace
13, rue des Beaux-Arts

Three years before his death on November 30, 1900, Oscar Wilde at last found relief from his financial difficulties by moving to this hotel. The hotel proprietor allowed the payment of the bill to lag, there were friends to turn to for loans, and restaurant owners ran bills for weeks or months. Wilde died just weeks before his forty-sixth birthday, in Room 16, now preserved with several pieces of the furniture that he used. Although the rent was only the equivalent of twelve dollars a day, he died as he had always lived—beyond his means.

The experiences of Thomas Wolfe in the years 1925 and 1926 when he stayed here provided material for his 1935 manuscript, *Of Time and the River.* The character Eugene Gant stopped at what was then Hotel d'Alsace. Like many other American expatriates, such as Ernest Hemingway, Wolfe received his mail at the Morgan Guaranty Trust Paris office in the Place Vendôme.

Continue on Rue des Beaux-Arts to the corner where directly in front you will see a large courtyard.

*Garden of Natalie Clifford Barney, 20, rue Jacob. Courtesy of
Felicity Leng.*

Thomas Wolfe and partial manuscript of Of Time and the River.
Courtesy of Charles Scribner's Art Archives.

27. Ecole des Beaux-Arts
14, rue Bonaparte

In the nineteenth century world of American architecture, it was important to study the baroque-style at the Ecole des Beaux-Arts. The famous designer Bernard Maybeck returned to teach at the University of California and encouraged Julia Morgan to attend the school. She was its first female student. The publisher William Randolph Hearst and his family later employed Maybeck and Morgan to design their California estates.

American architect Raymond Hood graduated from the school in 1911. With his partner John Mead Howells, Hood designed the Chicago Tribune Tower. In an article in *Architectural Forum,* Hood wrote that his Beaux-Arts teacher, Lalaux, in response to a student having trouble finding a suitable ornament for use in a particular place, remarked, "Why not try nothing?"

While attending a James M. Whistler exhibit here in 1905, Marcel Proust was so impressed by Whistler's landscapes that he sent a note to his mother telling her she should attend and enclosed a list of paintings he recommended she view. Whistler was already famous and had been made an Officier de la Légion d'Honneur. His painting, *The Artist's Mother,* had been sold to the French government and hung in the Musée Luxembourg.

28. Residence of Anatole France
15 and 19 quai Malaquais

When Anatole France died in 1924, the funeral procession from his home was described by "Genêt" (Janet Flanner):

". . .one of the biggest, most pretentious spectacles modern Paris has ever seen, with its vast display of flowers and detachments of troops assembled . . . outside the house . . . the cortège was followed through the streets by a . . . group of disrespectful Surrealists who despised his popularity and his literary style, and who shouted insults to his memory in unison the whole way. This was possibly the first of their sadistic street manifestations and was considered a scandal, since Paris has so long been noted [as] a great appreciator of its intellectual figures."

A soft-spoken, simple and kind man, France was awarded the 1921 Nobel Prize in Literature. Albert Einstein, when asked for his opinion of France, replied, "He is skeptical intellectually, but not sentimentally."

Continue on the quai to your first left, then turn left on Rue des Saints-Pères and follow it until you turn left again back on Rue Jacob.

29. Formerly Hôtel Jacob et d'Angleterre
44 rue Jacob

Upon arrival in Paris in 1921, Sherwood Anderson rented a room here for seventy-five cents a day. Anderson abandoned a career in advertising at the age of forty-four, and became an established writer with the publication of *Winesburg, Ohio.*

According to William Faulkner, Anderson was the father of his generation of American writers.

It was on Anderson's recommendation that Ernest and Hadley Hemingway stayed at this "good and cheap" hotel in December 1921. No longer cheap nowadays, it is a favorite of American publishers. On Christmas day, the Hemingways walked down Rue Bonaparte and across the Seine to Avenue de l'Opera for Christmas lunch at the *chic* Café de la Paix. The cost of the meal was more than they had estimated. Leaving Hadley as collateral, Hemingway had to walk back to Rue Jacob for more money.

Take your next left onto Rue Bonaparte again.

30. Formerly Grand Hôtel de la France
24, rue Bonaparte

Henry Miller and his wife June stayed here in April and May of 1928. In preparation for a bicycle tour of southern France, Miller was teaching her how to ride a bicycle, using the nearby short Rue Visconti as the practice route.

31. Le Pré aux Clercs
30, rue Bonaparte

Hemingway wrote to Sherwood Anderson that Le Pré aux Clercs had become their regular eating place. "Two can get a high grade dinner there with wine, à la carte, for twelve francs." The dollar was then valued at fourteen francs.

32. Hôtel St.-Germain-des-Prés
36, rue Bonaparte

In 1925, the young American writer Janet Flanner began a fifty-year residence in Paris. She agreed to write a letter from Paris for Harold Ross's new magazine, *The New Yorker.* More than seven hundred columns appeared under the pseudonym "Genêt." The letters are full of entertaining observations about French and European political, social, and artistic scenes.

Janet Flanner was a close friend of Hemingway. Perhaps, in perspective, they were drawn to each other because both of their fathers had committed suicide. Sitting at a rear table at the close-by Café aux Deux-Magots, they discussed suicide as an act of freedom. The talk ended with the mutual declaration that if either of them ever committed suicide, the other was not to grieve, but remember that liberty could be as important in the act of dying as in the act of living. Later, after Hemingway shot himself, Flanner wrote that she recognized his mortal act of gaining liberty, but that she grieved most because he died in a state of ruin.

Having returned to Paris to pursue a serious writing career, in February 1930, Henry Miller paid five hundred francs ($20) for a room five floors up. He wrote of Paris, "The streets sing, the stones talk. The houses drip history, glory and romance." In his early struggles to make money from his works, Miller thought Paris helped provide the stimulus for an entirely different way of life. Paris was the only place where an artist could remain an artist with dignity. "I was infuriated and intoxicated."

33. Rue Guillaume Apollinaire

In 1951, on the anniversary of Guillaume Apollinaire's death in 1918, a one block street between Rue Bonaparte and Rue St.-Benoit was named for the "Poet of Paris". Wilhelm Apollinaris de Kostrowitzky loved the streets of Paris, particularly St.-Germain-des-Prés area, with its narrow streets, busy markets, and convenient location. After he moved to the quarter in 1913 he would often be seen walking back to his former home in Montmartre. Usually accompanied by a friend, he was an indefatigable walker and as they moved and conversed he would point out historical landmarks; often they were examples of interesting architecture. Food and cooking also interested him, and he often observed the preparation in the exotic restaurants where he usually dined. Not only was Apollinaire a successful and important symbolist poet, he was also a keen art critic, writer of novels and stories and a brilliant conversationalist with a magnetic personality. Gertrude Stein believed that Apollinaire was the most vivid of the personalities surrounding Picasso. He was "extraordinarily brilliant and no matter what the subject, if he knew anything about it or not, he quickly saw the whole meaning."

34. Square Laurent Prache
Rue Bonaparte and Rue de l'Abbaye

Walk into and through the gardens of the Eglise St. Germain-des-Prés

The central bell tower at St. Germain-des-Prés is the oldest church structure in Paris, dating to the eleventh century. The square is the former site of a sixth-century Merovingian Abbey. Upon entering the gate, one can see directly in front Picasso's "Head of a Woman," created in 1959 and dedicated to his loyal friend Apollinaire. The bust is strong and unusual in the garden. In the winter the garden's starkness and the austere form of the church match the powerful lines of the sculpture.

Exit the garden and turn right down Rue de l'Abbaye, then take a left on Rue Cardinale.

35. Former Offices of Black Sun Press
2, rue Cardinale.

On the curve of the narrow street, a floor above printer Roger Lescaret, was the office of the Black Sun Press. Harry and Caresse Crosby chose the name from a poem by their friend Archibald MacLeish, "No Lamp Has Ever Shown Us Where To Look." The last lines are: "Still fixed upon the impenetrable skies/The small black circle of the sun." Crosby, a fanatical sun worshipper had a tattoo of the sun on the bottom of one foot. The finely made books were edited and designed by Caresse Crosby with Harry Crosby selecting the titles. They relished their lives as patrons of the arts and produced books by James Joyce, D. H. Lawrence, Ernest Hemingway, Ford Maddox Ford, and Archibald MacLeish. Harry's cousin, Walter Van Rensselaer Berry, willed him forty-seven letters from Henry James that were then published in volumes by the Press that existed in Paris until 1933. From 1936 until the fifties, Caresse Crosby edited or supervised its publication in the United States.

Round the corner to the Rue de Furstemberg. To your left you will see a small square.

36. Place de Furstemberg

Place de Furstemburg, centered by a single white-globed lamp and four paulownia trees, has excellent acoustics and is often the scene of impromptu concerts by street artists. Henry Miller's *Tropic of Cancer* describes the square as having ". . . the poetry of T. S. Eliot . . . very sterile, hybrid, full of forbidden longings."

Drop in at Number Six, the Musée Delacroix, the former atelier of Eugene Delacroix (1798-1863). While head of the romantic school in his day, his brilliant palette, use of lighting and feeling of movement would inspire the impressionists of the latter nineteenth century. He thus provided a strong foundation for modern art.

Exit the square on Rue de l'Abbaye, turn left, then right on Rue de l'Echaude, then turn right around the church to Place St.-Germain-des-Prés.

37. Café aux Deux-Magots
Place St.-Germain-des-Prés and Rue Bonaparte

According to Morley Callaghan, "St.-Germain-des-Prés with its three cafés—Lipp, Flore, and Deux Magots—was a focal point, the real Paris for industrious intellectuals. Painters and actors from other capitals, as well as expensive women, would to this neighborhood. André Gide used to dine at the Deux Magots. Picasso often passed by on the street. The Deux Magots, while remaining a neighborhood café, was a center of international Paris life.

From the terrace, step inside and examine the middle pillar of the café. The *deux magots* are the two wooden statues of Chinese dignitaries proclaiming the café's fortunate origins. A novelty shop was originally planned for this location, but before it could move here a bar opened and took the name.

Here, *transition* publisher Eugene Jolas introduced Harry and Caresse Crosby to Hart Crane. The Crosbys were excited by Crane's unfinished poem, *The Bridge,* and, to help him complete it, supported him at their country home just outside Paris. They also agreed to publish it. Although he managed to compose the "Cape Hatteras" part of his epic, Crane drank excessively and abusively, and was even imprisoned in July 1929 for punching a policeman. He was thrown into a prison cell where the rats bit him. After six months Crane was released into the custody of the American Embassy, and Crosby bought him a return ticket to New York.

The trio of Louis Aragon, André Breton and Philippe Soupault often sat at the café while formulating the *Surrealist Manifestos* (1924-1930). Other surrealists frequently joining them were André Masson, Max Ernst, Man Ray and Joan Miró.

> *". . .The surrealists had their own club table facing the door of the Deux Magots, from which vantage point a seated surrealist could conveniently insult any newcomer with whom he happened to be feuding, or discuss his plan to horsewhip an editor of some belligerent anti-surrealist newspaper for having mentioned his name or, worse, for having failed to mention it, in the latest surrealist gossip notes on the bitter power struggle between the devotees of surrealism's founder, André Breton, and their rivals, who had shifted to the leadership of Louis Aragon, surrealism's greatest novelist and prince of poets."*

—Janet Flanner

WALK

THE

ARISTOCRATIC

FAUBOURG

TWO

WALK II

Métro St.-Germain-des-Prés;
Buses 39, 48, 58, 63, 70.
From where it crosses Rue de Rennes, walk west on Blvd. St.-Germain to about the fourth door. Look for a sign depicting a large beer stein overflowing with suds.

1. Brasserie Lipp
151, blvd. St.-Germain

Walk II begins with lunch at the Alcasian brasserie so appetizingly described in Hemingway's *A Moveable Feast*:

". . . There were few people in the brasserie and when I sat down on the bench against the wall with the mirror in back and a table in front and the waiter asked if I wanted a beer I asked for a distingué, *the big glass mug that held a liter, and potato salad.*

"The beer was very cold and wonderful to drink. The pommes á l'huile were firm and marinated and the olive oil delicious. I ground black pepper over the potatoes and moistened the bread in the olive oil. After the first heavy draft of beer I drank and ate slowly. When the pommes á l'huile were gone, I ordered another serving and a cervalas. This was a sausage like a heavy, wide frankfurter split in two and covered with a special mustard sauce.

"I mopped up all the oil and all the sauce with bread and drank the beer slowly until it began to lose its coldness and then I finished it and ordered a demi and watched it drawn. It seemed colder than the distingué and I drank half of it."

Lipp's also serves sauerkraut and bratwurst. These days one is likely to find French politicians in its narrow recesses.

Follow the tree-lined boulevard St.-Germain west one and a half blocks, then turn left onto Rue des Saints-Pères.

2. Hôtel des Saints-Pères
65, rue des Saints-Pères

With a contract from *Vanity Fair* magazine to write two articles a month, Edna St. Vincent Millay arrived in Paris in January 1921. A recent graduate of Vassar College, Millay was already well known for her first book, *Renascence and Other Poems*. Since she wanted to build a career as a serious poet, Millay wrote the columns under an assumed name. She completed a five-act play, *The Lamp and the Bell,* for her alma mater, while living at this hotel.

In a letter to her sister, Millay wrote, "It is beautiful here even now. What will spring be? . . . I go out nearly every afternoon and walk miles and miles. It is so fascinating, when I once get started, that I can't stop."

3. Hôtel Pas-de-Calais
59, rue des Saints-Pères

During the summer of 1921, Ezra Pound (1885-1972) and his wife Dorothy Shakespear, an accomplished English artist, lived here in a top floor room Pound called his "roost." Considered the leader of the imagist school, Pound was then a contributing editor of *The Dial* and edited *Little Review* in Paris. He had recently arrived in Paris from London, utterly convinced that there was no intellectual life in England, and only in what he called "the Island of Paris" would he find acceptance of his brilliant and allusive poems.

In his early years as a writer, Ernest Hemingway submitted manuscripts for review to both Pound and Gertrude Stein. "Ezra was right half the time and when he was wrong he was so wrong you were never in doubt about it. Gertrude was always right."

Retrace your steps back to Blvd. St.-Germain. Cross to the other side and walk left for one block.

4. Residence of Guillaume Apollinaire
202, blvd. St.-Germain

The plaque on this building states that Guillaume Apollinaire lived here from 1913 until his death on 9 November 1918. Sixty-five meters above the Blvd. St.-Germain, on the sixth floor, the six small rooms with connecting hallways overlooked the neighboring roofs. Paintings, books, sculpture, mementos and an odd assortment of furniture filled the rooms. Apollinaire worked at a little desk placed in front of a window. He did most of the cooking in the miniscule kitchen. Today Apollinaire is considered to have been the major spokesman for the avant-garde movement in literature and the arts. His circle of friends included Picasso, André Derain, and Alfred Jarry, and he became the lover of the painter, Marie Laurencin. His writings showed his dedication to cubism and his constant support of the works of Georges Braque, Juan Gris, Fernand Léger, Francis Picabia, Henri Matisse and Marc Chagall. An article by Apollinaire, "Les Peintres Cubistes," coined the name of this vanguard movement.

Return to the first corner, then take a left and follow Rue St.-Guillaume for one block. Turn right on Rue Perronet and walk one block back east to Rue des Saints-Pères, and take another left. You will pass the site of the old Protestant cemetery; then cross the street on the right side, across Rue Jacob and continue north.

5. Residence of Rémy de Gourmant
29, rue des Saints-Pères

A prolific French writer of literary criticism, novels and verse, Rémy de Gourmant lived here near his close friend of five years, Natalie Clifford Barney. Because he was almost a recluse, Barney called on him first to seek his friendship. De Gourmont dedicated *Lettres à une Amazone* to the tall, accomplished equestrian. In 1918, she published *Pensées de l'Amazone*.

Return to the corner.

6. Formerly Restaurant Michaud
Rue des Saints-Pères and Rue Jacob

Ernest and Hadley Hemingway once stood outside this restaurant during their early and considerably lean years in Paris, reading the posted menu.

"Standing there I wondered how much of what we felt on the bridge was just hunger. I asked my wife and she said, 'I don't know, Tatie. There are so many kinds of hunger . . . memory is hunger.' "

In the twenties, you could find James Joyce and Ernest Hemingway dining here in their favorite restaurant. Hemingway described the Joyce family at dinner:

". . . he and his wife against the wall, Joyce peering at the menu through his thick glasses, holding the menu with one hand. Nora by him, a hearty but delicious eater, Georgio, thin and foppish, sleek-headed from the back, Lucia with heavy curly hair, a girl not yet grown, all of them talking Italian."

Cross Rue des Saints-Pères again and you will find upon turning right that Rue Jacob has become Rue de l'Université.

7. Formerly Hôtel l'Université
9, rue de l'Université

After learning about James Joyce from William Butler Yeats, Ezra Pound wrote to him in Trieste, where Joyce was teaching

Nora, George, and James Joyce in the early twenties. Courtesy of Princeton University Library, Sylvia Beach Collection.

Ezra Pound at window of Shakespeare and Company, 1920. Courtesy of Princeton University Library, Sylvia Beach Collection.

English at a Berlitz school to inquire about the possibility of publishing some of Joyce's work.

Five years later, in 1920, Pound financed the Joyce family's return to England. Wearing a secondhand suit and a new pair of shoes (purchased by Pound), Joyce, with his wife Nora and their son and daughter, stopped in Paris for a few days' visit, and stayed at a private pension in this building. The visit spanned twenty years, however, in the metropolis Joyce called "the last of the human cities."

Twenty-two-year-old poet and critic T. S. Eliot (1888-1965) spent the summer of 1910 here, when he was on the verge of becoming an employee of a London bank. Through the sponsorship of Lady Rothemere, Eliot escaped what would have been a regrettable fate and became editor of the English publication, *The Criterion*. Eliot's first important poem, *The Love Song of J. Alfred Prufrock* (1915), was composed during this period and brilliantly expresses the torment of unstable identity.

When Eliot finally met Stein in Paris in the fall of 1924, he had already become immensely influential as a critic. When he challenged Stein to explain her consistent use of the split infinitive, Stein replied, "Henry James." Eliot later agreed to publish a sample of her work, adding that he would only consider the most recent piece. That same evening Stein composed it for him: *A Description of the Fifteenth of November: A Portrait of T. S. Eliot.*

In 1948, Eliot received the Nobel Prize in Literature for his highly acclaimed, jazzy poetry. Afterward a friend said to him, "Congratulations on the prize, old boy. It's high time, I would say." Eliot gloomily replied, "It's too soon, I would say. The Nobel is a ticket to one's own funeral. No one has ever done anything after he got it."

When Eliot stayed here he read the French novel *Bubu of Montparnasse* and when the Black Sun Press published the English translation by Lawrence Vail in 1932, Eliot wrote the complimentary introduction. To him the book symbolized Paris as he had first known it.

Continue northwest along Rue d l'Université and go right on Rue de Beaune and walk two blocks to Rue de Lille. Turn left at the Rue de Lille.

8. Hôtel Elysée
9, rue de Beaune

During the time that Ezra Pound helped the Joyce family settle in Paris, he aided other young writers by promoting their works in *Poetry, The Dial* and *Little Review.* Pound was every inch the poet, with his velvet coat, open shirt with Danton collar, golden beard and long hair.

Following an insignificant accident in which Pound broke a chair at her house, Gertrude Stein ended her friendship with him. Much later she met the poet in the Jardin du Luxembourg and Pound inquired about coming around to see her. Stein replied that Alice had a bad toothache, and they would be busy picking wildflowers.

9. Site of Paul Rosenberg Galerie
Rue de Beaune

In the thirties, Paul Rosenberg represented Picasso's works in his gallery somewhere along this street. Picasso had begun yet another new period of expressionistic distortion, but in 1937 the German bombing of the Basque capitol, Guernica, inspired in him an unprecedented campaign against human destruction.

For the annual exhibit, *Rosenberg 1939,* Picasso painted twenty pictures of flowers in a vase. Rosenberg sold the flower paintings for 150,000 francs each. Privately Picasso had returned to painting roosters.

It was also here that the surrealist neo-pagan composer Erik Satie performed his works at avant-garde poetry and music events.

Walk southeast down Rue de Lille.

10. Residence of Harry and Caresse Crosby
19, rue de Lille

In this fine example of an eighteenth-century *hôtel-particulier,* one wing of three floors belonged to Harry and Caresse Crosby. Notice the huge wood door of the high wall, between two carved columns, each column topped with an urn overflowing with sandstone fruit and a garland of chiseled flowers. Usually open, it is possible to walk into the courtyard. Crosby's massive library on the top floor ran the length of the wing with three windows overlooking the street. The high-ceilinged, large rooms contained handworked wood trim and cut crystal chandeliers. The lavishly furnished formal drawing room was seldom used.

The Crosbys preferred bedroom and bathroom for their primary living areas.

The Crosbys usually retired to the bedroom at eight o'clock in the evening. Harry loved to read, write, work, eat and also entertain groups of friends in his bedroom. Adjoining the bedroom, the black and white bathroom contained a sunken marble tub. The room had an open fireplace, white bear-skin rug, and a cushioned chaise lounge. Guests bathing in the three-person tub were provided with an assortment of exotic bath oils, salts and thick robes. They were also invited to join the hosts in bed.

In 1938 the wing's occupants were surrealist Max Ernst and his wife Dorothy Tanning. Ernst was a longtime friend of the Crosbys. Ernst's *Misfortunes of the Immortals*, written with Paul Elouard and translated by Hugh Chisolm, was one of the final publications edited by Caresse Crosby in New York.

Many unusual oil paintings and collages by Ernst made noteworthy art news in the twenties. He created collage "glueings" by cutting pictures out of old mail order catalogues and and glueing them into original designs, which he later sold for high prices.

Continue down Rue de Lille to the next right, then walk to the end of narrow Rue Allent. At Rue de Verneuil once more, turn left.

11. Former Offices of *transition*
6, rue de Verneuil

In 1927, Eugene Jolas created the literary review *transition* in an apartment here next to the pretty garden. Here fellow Paris *Tribune* staff members Elliot Paul and Ned Calmer co-edited the magazine. Through a series of interviews from 1924 to 1926, Jolas introduced the works of the early surrealists to the English-speaking literary world. *Transition* represented the surrealist movement and printed works by André Gide and Philippe Soupault, and, in later years, works of Gertrude Stein, Archibald MacLeish, and Kay Boyle, among others. Wrote Jolas, "It is the artist's search for magic in this strange world about us that *transition* desires to encourage."

Continue down the Rue de Verneuil to Rue des Saints-Pères once more, and turn left toward the river. At Quai Voltaire turn left again.

Residence of Harry and Caresse Crosby, 19, rue de Lille. Courtesy of Felicity Leng.

53, rue de Varenne circa *1910. Courtesy of the Harvard University Libraries.*

12. Residence of Virgil Thomson, Paul Bowles, and Lucie Delarue-Mardrus
17, quai Voltaire

In 1925 the modern American composer George Antheil brought fellow composer Virgil Thomson to a Stein salon. During the ensuing long friendship, they developed a mutual respect for each other. According to Alice B. Toklas, he was intelligent, sensitive and witty. While a student at Harvard, Thomson had read Stein's *Tender Buttons* which he later wrote "changed my life."

During the thirteen years Thomson lived in the small attic room here beginning in 1927, he collaborated with Stein and composed the music for her opera *Four Saints in Three Acts*. On Friday afternoons, in his studio where only a tiny piece of the Seine is visible from the single window, Thomson would hold parties attended by such luminaries as Pablo Picasso, Jean Cocteau, André Gide, Christian Dior (then an art dealer), Ernest Hemingway and F. Scott Fitzgerald.

"Even the police treated you well if you were an artist," Virgil Thomson said of living in Paris. When he returned to New York in 1940 he became the music critic for the New York *Herald Tribune*.

In 1931 Paul Bowles lived here in another studio. During part of that time the impoverished painter Maurice Grossner shared the small space. They both liked to cook and served excellent simple meals to their friends.

Before he ran away from college in Virginia to live in Paris, Paul Bowles corresponded with Gertrude Stein. Stein had helped to promote his poems in continental publications, and she and Toklas assumed Bowles to be a genteel older man. The summer that Aaron Copland took him to meet her Stein was astonished to discover that Paul Bowles was a precocious young man of nineteen. The young Bowles had come to Paris to study musical composition, but at the time he lived here his writings were published in the many small publications such as *This Quarter*. It was Gertrude Stein who suggested that Bowles should move to Morocco and write. During the next fifty years Bowles wrote a number of novels and stories set in North Africa, including *The Sheltering Sky*.

Once in New York in 1934, Bowles wrote to Stein about the popularity of her new opera: "People walking on Broadway and sitting in Automats talked of 'The Saints Play' and usually sound doubtful as to whether it would be worthwhile trying to get tickets for it."

After her divorce from orientalist Dr. Joseph Delarue-Mardrus, French poet Lucie Delarue-Mardrus lived here from 1915 to 1936. Delarue-Mardrus was a gifted writer. Her novel, *L'Ange et les pervers* (1930), recalls her one-time love affair with Natalie Clifford Barney and the life to which she was introduced. The affair was followed by a long and deep friendship.

13. Hotel du Quai Voltaire
19, quai Voltaire

Willa Cather lived here for two months in 1920 while at work on her Pulitzer Prize (1922) novel, *One of Ours,* which was set in Paris.

Continue past *chic* antique shops and art galleries to Pont Royal. Turn left on Rue du Bac and walk a bit more than four blocks. Cross Rue Montalembert beyond which is the church of St.-Thomas-d'Aquin. Enter the rear door of the church and pass through to Place St.-Thomas-d'Aquin.

14. Eglise St.-Thomas-d'Aquin
Rue de Bac and Rue Montalembert

Enter the rear door of the church and walk through to the Place St.-Thomas-d'Aquin. Within a six-month period in 1918, in May and November, this church was the setting for the third marriage and, soon thereafter, the funeral of Guillaume Apollinaire. With Picasso and art dealer Ambrose Vollard as witnesses, Apollinaire married his third wife, Jacqueline "Ruby" Kolb in March 1918. In December of 1914, Apollinaire joined the French Army. He suffered a head wound during the war, but died of influenza on November 9, 1918. The funeral cortege wound from here through Paris streets decorated for the Armistice on November 11.

An editor of a number of reviews, Apollinaire published satirical and semi-pornographic pieces. He proclaimed that the writings of the Marquis de Sade would dominate the twentieth century. Wrote Gertrude Stein, "He always had a quality of keeping people together and, now that he was gone, everybody ceased to be friends."

Continue one block on the Rue St.-Thomas-d'Aquin, cross Blvd. St.-Germain, turn right and walk for one block. Turn left onto Blvd. Raspail.

15. Residence of James Joyce
5, blvd. Raspail

After living in three borrowed flats, in 1920 the family of James Joyce occupied this expensive flat. As usual, Joyce was living beyond his means, and his friends had to subsidize the rent. For instance, to furnish the new home, Joyce needed a *square* table to write on. The rooms were said to be tidy but very unimaginatively furnished. The living room had walls papered in a brown pattern and was graced with an upright piano and a goldfish bowl. The only picture in the room, a portrait of Joyce's father, was hung over the fireplace.

The elevator in the building's main entrance hall only held two riders. One day Joyce, Robert McAlmon and Morley Callaghan all rode up in it together. As it slowly ascended with the three men standing so close together, Joyce remarked, "I think what a loss to English literature if the lift fails and the three of us are killed."

Continue quite a distance down Blvd. Raspail until you come to the Rue de Sèvres intersection.

16. Hôtel Lutétia
43-45 blvd. Raspail

The roccoco façade is easy to spot. Picasso married Russian ballet dancer Olga Khaklova in the Russian Orthodox church in July 1918 and they honeymooned here at the Lutétia. After the marriage, the Picassos led an upper middle class life; he was now renowned and socialized with the *bourgeoisie* of Paris during what is now called his social butterfly period. He exchanged paint-stained corduroys for a dinner jacket and regularly attended soirées at the Right Bank townhouse of designer Coco Chanel. Here he mixed with art patrons and the *nouveau riche*. "Picasso is still doing beautiful work, when he has time," wrote Spanish artist Juan Gris during this period.

Two American authors stayed here for a short time when they first arrived in Paris. In January 1924, William Carlos Williams, a doctor from Rutherford, New Jersey, came to Paris to write poetry, for which he would someday be considered among the best modern American poets. He was introduced to Gertrude Stein by Robert McAlmon. Asking Williams what he would do if he had her many unpublished manuscripts, he replied tactlessly that he would pick out the best and burn the rest. Stein was shocked and replied, "No doubt. But then writing is not your *métier* (craft)." According to McAlmon, Williams retorted to Stein, who had attended four years at Johns Hopkins School of Medicine, and failed her last exams, "But, Doctor Stein, are you sure writing is *your* métier?"

In 1926, the American novelist Nathanael West, at the age of twenty-three, spent only a few days here while hunting for an even more humble room.

While writing her memoirs, *My Life,* in 1925, Isadora Duncan learned of the suicide of her husband, the Russian poet Cherque Essenin. They had never been divorced because of Duncan's belief that she made a vulgar gesture by marrying, and would not now make another by divorcing. As his widow, Duncan inherited his entire estate but gave the money to Essenin's mother and sister.

Cross Blvd. Raspail and continue right, past Square Boucicaut. Backtrack two blocks until you are back at Rue de Varenne. Along the way look for the Bon Marché store on the street behind the square. Alice B. Toklas purchased linen here. Turn left on Rue de Varenne. Pass the Italian embassy. Many state police are in evidence in the surrounding area because of nearby Hôtel Matignan, the offices of the premier of France.

17. Residence of Edith Wharton and Walter van Rensselaer Berry
53, rue de Varenne

Born in New York of aristocratic, wealthy parents, Edith Wharton was already a successful novelist with a large independent income, and when she decided to settle permanently in Paris, she maintained a large formal flat in this regal mansion. Her prolific career spanned thirty years. *House of Mirth* was published in 1905 and while living here she wrote *Ethan Frome.* The Pulitzer Prize was awarded for *Age of Innocence* and Wharton was the first woman to receive the gold medal of the National Institute of Arts and Letters.

With her dignified appearance and reserved manner, Wharton reflected the nineteenth-century manneredness of her friend Henry James rather than the early twentieth century of fellow

Edith Wharton circa *1905. Courtesy of the Harvard University Libraries.*

American expatriates. At the age of sixty in 1922, she had tried valiantly to read *Ulysses,* but finally dismissed it as "a welter of pornography, unformed and unimportant drivel," a sentiment shared by many of her contemporaries in the literary establishment. In her letters, papers and memoirs of 1934, *A Backward Glance,* Wharton discreetly revealed a sensuous nature underneath the cold façade and stylish gowns. A woman with a brilliant mind, but also exceedingly shy, the largesse of her emotions went into her books.

The apartment consisted of a round library containing all the works of Henry James, who often came to visit and a marble bust of the novelist. Wharton and James wrote books that judged and described the sins of their upper-class society. A high-ceilinged drawing room, elegant dining room, good-sized kitchen, six bedrooms, another smaller sitting room, a couple of out-of-date bathrooms, bedroom, and guest suite and bath completed this immense home.

After the First World War, Wharton wrote that Paris had become,

". . . simply awful—a kind of earthquake of motors, buses, trams, lorries, taxis and other howling and swooping and colliding engines, with hundreds of thousands of United States citizens rushing about in them and tumbling out at one's door."

Describing the "new American cad," she said, "All that I thought American in a true sense is gone, and I see nothing but vainglory, crassness and total ignorance."

After Wharton moved to the village of St. Brice-sous-Forêt twelve miles north of Paris in 1919, Walter Van Rensselaer Berry, second cousin and surrogate father to Harry Crosby, moved into the rooms in this seventeenth-century *hôtel-particulier.* The dapper Berry was born and raised in Paris, educated at Harvard and returned to France as a lawyer. From 1916 to 1919, he acted as president of the Paris American Chamber of Commerce.

Edith Newbold Jones and Berry had had a brief summer romance in Newport before her marriage to Edward Wharton, and in the years that followed they remained close friends. After the Whartons divorced, a number of acquaintances expected Berry to propose to Wharton, but the dilettante bachelor continued to enjoy the company of numerous other companions. Wharton *did* credit him as her literary mentor.

When Berry died in 1927, Harry Crosby was named the executor of the estate. The will stipulated that Berry's valuable library was to be offered first to Wharton for her choice of the books she wanted to keep. After much bickering between the two, she finally chose very few books, and the remaining books were moved to the magnificent Crosby library on the Rue de Lille.

Although she associated with French nobility and extremely wealthy Europeans, Wharton always remained a nineteenth-century American in her conduct, manners and habits. Christmas meant a dinner of roast turkey and steamed plum pudding with close American friends.

18. Residence of Edith Wharton
58, rue de Varenne

The Whartons' first home in Paris, in January 1907, was an apartment here in what is now another government building in this quarter, Faubourg St.-Germain. The seventh arrondissement was populated by nobility. The narrow tree-lined avenues are still faced by the high walls protecting the grand hotels. Many are now foreign embassies and official French government offices.

The Whartons leased the majestic rooms here from George Vanderbilt in time to celebrate Edith Wharton's forty-fifth birthday. The drawing room floor was covered by a crimson Aubusson carpet and the majestic rooms contained charming old furniture, antique Chinese porcelains and fine bronzes. Accompanying the Whartons to Paris were six servants and two dogs.

Edward Wharton was a handsome member of a prominent Boston family. The proper and aristocratic American couple often presided at large formal parties and were accepted into the social life of the grand salons of their neighbors.

It was in Edith Wharton's relationships with other men such as Walter Berry, Morton Fullerton and Henry James that she showed the warmth she rarely displayed publicly. The "Dearest Edith" letters of Henry James reveal the depth of their platonic devotion to each other.

Just after the Hôtel Matignon, turn left at the corner onto Rue Vaneau, walk past the high white wall and black doors of the Syrian embassy, onto Rue de Chanaleilles on your right. Continue up Rue de Chanaleilles to where it meets Rue Barbet-de-Jouy, then left past the Tunisian embassy to Rue de Babylone. Walk right one block, then left onto Rue Monsieur.

On the corner of Rue Babylone and Rue Monsieur is a curious oriental garden and building housing a theater. In 1897 the authentic pagoda was moved from Japan by Alain Morin, founder of the Bon Marché store, for his wife, an actress. She presented theatrical performances and costume balls in her private theater. In 1931 it was converted to a cinema.

19. Residence of Cole Porter
13, rue Monsieur

In the heart of the aristocratic faubourg, the successful composer Cole Porter and his wife Linda Lee lived here from 1919 to 1939. Both of them had large independent incomes and they lived in a lavishly furnished apartment. In one room were red chairs lined with red kid next to walls of zebra skins. Another room had walls covered with platinum paper.

The American sewing machine heiress, Princess Winaretta Singer de Polignac, sister of Isaac Singer, commissioned Porter to compose a jazz ballet. When "Within the Quota" premiered in 1923 at the Théâtre de Champs-Elysées, it was a great success. Porter was at the piano in 1924 when George Gershwin's "Rhapsody in Blue" was first auditioned in Paris. Gershwin stayed in a Right Bank hotel in 1928 while composing *An American in Paris,* a concerto inspired by the atmosphere and street noises of the city.

Return to Rue Babylone, turn left, and then right onto Blvd. des Invalides.

20. Residence of Henri Matisse
33, blvd. des Invalides

The Matisse family, including the two sons who had been living with their grandparents, moved into this former convent with low-rent rooms that included a large studio. Some of Henri Matisse's followers, such as Sarah (Sally) Stein, sister-in-law of Gertrude Stein, encouraged him to conduct classes in painting and sculpture. The students of the Matisse Academy came from many countries and were varied in their interests and abilities. Sally Stein and Max Weber joined the first class. When Matisse met with his loosely organized class on Saturday, the students

Cole Porter. Courtesy of the International Museum of Photography at George Eastman House.

vied for the attention of *Cher Maître,* as Gertrude Stein called him, and quarrelled often and loudly.

It was at the 1908 Salon des Indépendants that Matisse, upon viewing some of the paintings, exclaimed, *"Mais c'est du cubisme!* (But this is Cubism!)"

Follow the Blvd. des Invalides with the gardens of the museum on your right. Within the tall iron fence Auguste Rodin's statuary is displayed among the trees and walks. At the corner of Rue de Varenne turn right.

21. Musée Rodin
77, rue de Varenne

The former Hôtel de Biron, constructed in 1731, was a magnificent private residence. In 1908, the Catholic Church acquired the building and large surrounding gardens for use as a boarding school, or *pensionnat.* Isadora Duncan and Auguste Rodin worked in private rooms here. When the French government purchased the property in 1910, Rodin was granted permission to continue his studio on the condition that he leave his works to the state.

The poet Rainer Maria Rïlke also stayed here while serving as the unpaid secretary to Rodin. Born in 1875, he was to become one of the foremost European poets of this generation in Europe and an inspiration for poets worldwide.

American sculptor Malvina Hoffman worked as an assistant to Rodin from 1910 until he died in 1917. Rodin was described by Isadora Duncan as "short, square powerful with a close-cropped head and plentiful beard. He showed his works with the simplicity of the great."

The fine Rodin collection is on display inside the musée and in the garden where "The Thinker" is seated. (Walk II is purposely short to allow time to visit two important museums.)

Upon exiting the museum, proceed right or southward. Cross the street to take your first left onto Rue Bourgogne. Go two blocks and turn right onto Rue Las Cases. Walk past the Basilica de Ste.-Clotilde on your right and a lovely neighborhood park on your left.

22. Residence of Archibald MacLeish
23, rue Las Cases

The poet Archibald MacLeish, his wife and two children, arrived in Paris in September 1923. MacLeish had just rejected an offer of employment from a prestigious New England law firm in order to live in France and write poetry. For ten months the family stayed in this apartment while MacLeish worked on the poem *Einstein,* which was later published in *Streets of the Moon* (1926). He described their small abode:

> *"It has a little salon adequate for about four people at a time, a dining room only slightly larger than the ordinary stomach, one decent-sized bedroom, two small ones, a tiny bathroom and a cell-like 'horror' and a bit of a hall."*

Proceed along Rue Las Cases to the Rue de Bellechase. Make a left and continue to the Seine and the Place Henry de Montherlant, opposite the Tuileries.

23. Musée d'Orsay
1, rue de Bellechasse

The iron and glass vaulted 150-yard-long hall was once the Gare d'Orsay, the grandest railroad station in France. Opened on Bastille Day 1900 for the World Exposition, it served as the central rail terminal for trains from the southwest. Resembling a fine arts palace, the ornate limestone building encompassed a fashionable hotel.

By 1935 twentieth-century progress made its short platforms useless for the longer trains and the French national railway closed the station in 1939. The elegant hotel existed until 1973. It was in the ballroom of the hotel that General Charles de Gaulle held his famous press conference on May 19, 1958, announcing his return to power. The former restaurant of the hotel is open again for lunch and dinner. It is a trip to the past to dine in the grand, ornately mirrored room bejewelled with the original sparkling crystal chandeliers.

As you enter the eight-story high glass nave that formerly held two railroad tracks, the 17,200 square meters of exhibition space will stun you. The glorious impressionist collection is hung in a top floor gallery. The museum also holds the finest examples of painting, sculpture, architecture and photography from the period 1848-1914. These include 2,300 paintings (700 of which are impressionist works), 250 pastels, 1,500 sculptures, 13,000 photographs, innumerable examples of architecture, 1,100 miscellaneous objects d'art of the decorative arts, film, posters and media.

Tours are given in English every day at 11:30 A.M.. It will help to orient you around the building and introduce the enormous collection. *C'est trés magnifique!*

WALK

THE SPIRIT OF ODEONIA

THREE

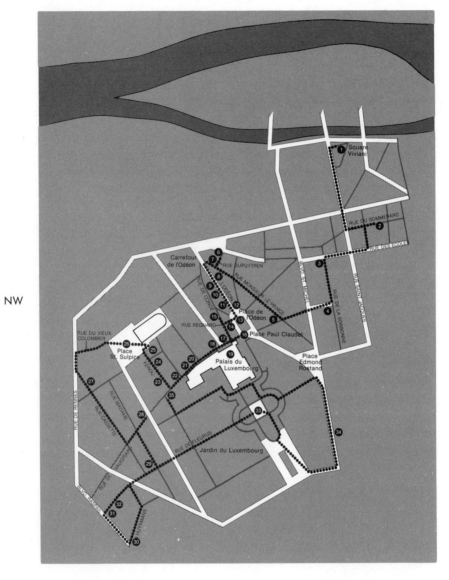

SW

WALK III

Métro St.-Michel; Buses: 24, 27, 47, 63, 86, 87

From Place St.-Michel, begin this tour by following Rue de la Huchette east across Rue St.-Jacques, and visit the home of the new Shakespeare and Company bookshop.

1. Shakespeare and Company
37, rue de la Bûcherie

Walk III begins at a bookshop named Shakespeare and Company, which has no relationship to the original founded by Sylvia Beach. This often crowded, densely-filled shop was opened in 1964 by George Whitman, who does not claim kinship to the nineteenth-century poet, Walt Whitman, who also ran a bookstore in Brooklyn, New York. Now a French citizen, Whitman notes, "It has been said that perhaps no man liked so many things, and disliked so few as Walt Whitman, and I at least aspire to the same modest attainment." He has remarked that the bookstore will continue, in a threatening world, "to be a refuge for writers and bibliophiles inspired by the same ideal as Sylvia Beach."

Return to the corner of Rue St.-Jacques, turn left and walk several blocks west, crossing Blvd. St.-Germain. At the next corner turn left onto Rue Sommerard.

2. Hôtel Marignan
13, rue Sommerard

In the early years of the First World War, many young American would-be writers, intellectuals and college students joined the French forces as volunteer ambulance drivers. In a letter written home to a friend, the poet e.e. cummings objected to the strict discipline of the Norton-Harjes Ambulance Corps. The letter was intercepted by the French censors and cummings was charged with treasonable correspondence. When "queried" by his bullying interrogators, who asked "Do you hate the Krauts?" cummings answered, "No, I love the French." He was locked in a French military prison for six months until family pressure secured his release and he returned to Boston.

Back home, the son of a New England Unitarian minister once again, cummings wrote to his close friend, John Dos Passos, whom he had met at Harvard, that he was restless and longed to return to Paris. In 1921 he finally did and came directly to this small hotel located in the area lived in by students of the

George Whitman with French student in front of the Shakespeare and Company Bookshop, 37, rue de la Bûcherie. Courtesy of Felicity Leng.

Sorbonne. Cummings painted, wrote poetry, plays and completed his first book, *The Enormous Room (1922),* which describes his prison experiences.

In the spirit of Apollinaire's experimental compositions, e.e. cummings' poems are famous for their altered punctuation and spelling, and verses that refuse to be bullied by traditional rules of meter and rhyme.

Backtrack up Rue Sommerard to Rue Thenard, and with the school on your left, turn onto Rue des Ecoles. Walk two blocks to a sign with a foaming beer stein.

3. Brasserie Balzar
49, rue des Ecoles

Like hundreds of French brasseries in appearance, the Balzar in the twenties was believed by newspaperman William L. Shirer to have the finest food in Paris. James Thurber and Elliot Paul, fellow writers on the *Tribune* often joined him.

Upon exiting the Balzar, take a right and continue south on Rue de la Sorbonne. You will climb Mt. Ste.-Geneviève, past several small bookshops to Place de la Sorbonne, a lovely square lined with lime trees and benches.

4. Hôtel Sélect
1 Place de la Sorbonne

New Zealand short story writer Katherine Mansfield moved to Paris in 1918 after several unhappy years in Germany. Her room and board here cost ten francs, about fifty cents a day. Diagnosed with fatal tuberculosis, Mansfield was desperately seeking a cure and eventually fell under the influence of two Russian occult gurus promising her a miraculous recovery. Seeking religious enlightenment and bodily health, she entered a commune in Fontainebleau, and died there in January 1923. *Bliss and Other Stories* (1920) and *The Garden Party and Other Stories* showed brilliant promise, but only after her death did Mansfield's stories achieve wide readership.

Almost twenty years later in 1937, twenty-five-year-old Eric Sevareid paid the same amount for his room. He was then writing for the Paris *Herald,* the European edition of the New York *Herald Tribune.* With war clouds threatening all of Europe in 1938, in a rare interview with Gertrude Stein, he questioned her about the possibility of Hitler's threats leading to a war. ''Hitler will never go to war," she replied. "He is not the dangerous one . . . No, Mussolini—there's the dangerous man."

In 1939, Sevareid left the position of daytime city editor to join CBS radio in London. His broadcasts made him one of the most familiar commentators of World War II.

Exit Place de la Sorbonne on the Blvd. St.-Michel side and cross the Blvd. to the Rue Vaugirard. Then walk about one and a half blocks.

5. Formerly Hôtel de Lisbonne
4, rue de Vaugirard

With its proximity to the nearby Balzar, this hotel was a favorite of the Paris *Tribune* staff. When William L. Shirer lived here in September 1925, his large room was furnished with a writing table, dresser, bookcase and a comfortable double bed. Since the building did not contain a bathroom, the bidet served as bathtub and a washbasin stood below a large mirror. Good light was provided by elegant floor-to-ceiling French windows. All of this cost the equivalent of ten dollars a month.

Edgar (Ned) Calmer, a journalist and friend of Hemingway, wrote for both the *Herald* and the *Tribune* during his stay here from 1927 to 1934. In his novel, *All the Summer Days (1961),* he describes life at this hotel.

When, in 1933, Hemingway discovered that Calmer's two-year-old daughter had not been baptized in the Catholic Church, he insisted that Calmer should correct the matter immediately. Within a few days the ceremony took place and Hemingway served as godfather. Hemingway claimed to have been baptized a Catholic on an Italian battlefield.

A year later, Hemingway nominated Calmer for a Guggenheim Grant but the motion was rejected. Hemingway later admitted that no one he had nominated was ever accepted.

Backtrack down Rue Vaugirard to the corner and turn left onto Rue Monsieur le Prince, for about three blocks, turning right on Rue Dupuytren.

6. Original Location of Shakespeare and Company
8, rue Dupuytren

In the middle of the block on the left is the original home of Shakespeare and Company. It is here that Sylvia Beach, daughter of a Presbyterian minister in Princeton, New Jersey, opened the shop on 17 November 1919.

While studying French literature at the Sorbonne, Beach formed a lifelong friendship with Adrienne Monnier, owner of La Maison des Amis des Livres, a French bookshop, lending library and poetry center. Monnier found a former laundry at this location, just around the corner from her store, and thought that it would be most appropriate. In her book, *Shakespeare and Company,* Beach describes the day Monnier showed her the premises:

". . . at number 8—there were only about ten numbers on this hilly little street—was a shop with the shutters up and a sign reading, Boutique à louer. *'It had once been a laundry,' said Adrienne, pointing to the words,* gros *and* fin, *on either side of the door, meaning they did both sheets and fine linen. Adrienne, who was rather plump, placed herself under the* gros *and told me to stand under the* fin. *'That's you and me,' she said."*

The first customers were French, inherited from Monnier's venture. Students and professors from the nearby Sorbonne supported the lending library. French writers Léon-Paul Fargue, Valéry Larbaud, André Gide and Jules Romains were visitors to the shop in the first few days and they remained its faithful friends for twenty-two years. One of the shop's most faithful patrons was a young philosophy student and teacher, Simone de Beauvoir, who joined in 1935 and borrowed many American titles. Thanks to de Beauvoir and her companions, Jean-Paul Sartre and André Malraux, authors such as William Faulkner and John Dos Passos gained critical acclaim in Europe before they were appreciated in America.

Records show that Gertrude Stein's claim of being the first annual subscriber to the lending library is incorrect. When Stein joined there were already ninety members, several of whom were annual members. Beach published James Joyce's *Ulysses* in March 1922, and afterwards Stein did not renew her subscription. Stein viewed Joyce as a rival literary innovator and refused to admit he was her equal. She considered Beach to be disloyal for shepherding Joyce and the novel *Ulysses.* Stein eventually moved her library business to the American Library.

Beach declared that "Gertrude's subscription was merely a friendly gesture. She took little interest in any but her own books." Leo Stein was a more active member of the lending library.

Walk back onto Rue Monsieur-le-Prince to the stunning, large carved wooden doors at the top and turn right and continue your promenade to the right onto the Carrefour l'Odéon.

7. Formerly Offices of *Gargoyle*
15 Carrefour de l' Odéon

Henry James called Odéonia (Monnier's name for the area) "the great literary workshop of Paris."

In a small building facing the circle at the bottom of Rue de l'Odéon, *Gargoyle* (1921-22), the first English language expatriate magazine in Europe, was published here by Gilliam and Moss, an American couple. Arthur Moss and Florence Gilliam wrote on the goings-on of the Paris crowd and generally on European life. Malcolm Cowley called the magazine "Greenwich Village in Montparnasse." According to|Archibald MacLeish,

> *"Turning up from St.-Germain to go home past the bottoms of the gardens to the Boulevard St.-Michel, one kept Shakespeare and Company to the starboard and Adrienne Monnier's Amis des Livres to port, and felt, as one rose with the tide toward the* théâtre, *that one had passed the gates of a dream . . . It was enough for a confused young lawyer in a grand and vivid time to look from one side to the other and say to himself, as the cold came up from the river, Gide was here on Thursday and Monday Joyce was there."*

Bearing left, enter the Rue de l'Odéon.

8. Formerly La Maison des Amis des Livres
7, rue de l'Odéon

Above the entrance of this former bookshop hangs a wrought-iron sculpture depicting Joyce and Monnier walking side by side, above the words, *La Pensée Sauvage (Savage Mind)*. The sculpture was done from a photograph taken as they passed near the exact spot under which the sign now hangs. It was taken by Monnier's friend, the sociologist and photographer Gisèle Freund. *La Pensée Sauvage* is the title of a famous work by Claude Lévi-Strauss, a celebrated French anthropologist. The friendship that developed between Freund, Monnier, and Sylvia Beach after 1935 resulted in Freund's photography of lesser known friends of the two women—people who later became famous writers and artists. In 1915, Monnier opened what was quickly to become a meeting place for elite French writers. She confessed to Freund that she became a bookseller in order to read the books she couldn't afford to purchase. The book-lined walls of the lending library encompassed the setting for readings by André Gide, Paul Valéry, André Breton and Valéry Larbaud. From the shop, Monnier published the literary review, *Gazette des Amis des Livres,* and its successor, *Navire d'Argent.*

When Sylvia Beach first entered the shop in 1917, she saw Adrienne Monnier, a chubby twenty-six-year-old Frenchwoman who warmly greeted her. Beach wrote of Monnier's appearance,

"Most striking were her eyes. They were blue-grey and slightly bulging . . . she looked alive. Her dress . . . a long, full skirt down to her feet and a sort of tight-fitting velvet waistcoat over a white silk blouse. She was in grey and white like her bookshop."

Until Monnier's death in 1955, she and Beach not only shared the fortune of living on Rue de l'Odéon, but also their love of literature and their support of young writers—French, British and American. They created what Joyce christened "Stratford-on-Odéon."

9. Residence of Robert McAlmon
8, rue de l'Odéon

From 1922 to 1926, this was the first home of Robert McAlmon's Contact Editions. Robert McAlmon edited the manuscripts in his apartment and William Bird printed the limited-editions, fine books on a seventeenth-century hand-press. McAlmon used Shakespeare and Company as his mail box. Limited to three hundred copies of works that McAlmon stated ". . . were not likely to be published by other publishers for commercial or legislative reasons," the collection of works included William Carlos Williams' *Spring and All* (1922), Ernest Hemingway's first book, *Three Stories and Ten Poems* (1923), and Gertrude Stein's *The Making of Americans* (1925).

The friendship of McAlmon and Stein ended in 1925; he claimed she had meddled with the distribution of her book. McAlmon credited Stein with the statement: "Nobody has done anything to develop the English language since Shakespeare, except myself, and Henry James perhaps a little."

James Joyce and Adrienne Monnier on Rue de l'Odéon, 1938.
Courtesy of Gisèle Freund.

Sylvia Beach and Steven Vincent Benét in front of Shakespeare and Company, Rue Dupuytren. Courtesy of Princeton University Library, Sylvia Beach Collection.

Although he composed essays and poetry, McAlmon's primary influence on the modern literary period was as a publisher. Drinking heavily and frequenting the bars and cafés of Paris night life also filled much of his time.

10. Second Home of the Original Shakespeare and Company, 12, rue de l'Odéon

The original wood-faced front has been removed from the now-empty space. It formerly looked similar to Number 10.

For the English writer, Bryher Ellerman, then the wife of Robert McAlmon:

> *"There was only one street in Paris for me, the Rue de l'Odéon. It is association, I suppose, but I have always considered it one of the most beautiful streets in the world. It meant, naturally, Sylvia and Adrienne and the happy hours I spent in their libraries. Has there ever been another bookshop like Shakespeare and Co.? It was not just crowded shelves, it was Sylvia herself, standing like a passenger from the Mayflower with the wind still blowing through her hair and a thorough command of French slang, waiting to help us and be our guide."*

To the left of the final home of Shakespeare and Company were a shoemaker, a corsetmaker and an appraiser of libraries and book auctions. On the right, an orthopedic shoemaker, a music shop and a nose-spray manufacturer. The 1921 move gave Beach a larger space plus two small rooms above. A large stove sitting in front of the hearth warmed visitors and readers. The space above the mantel was crowded with photos of contemporary writers. American expatriates used the shop as a Left-Bank American Express, to receive the mail that was piled on the mantel. From a large desk-table, Beach enthusiastically greeted visitors and listened for the latest literary gossip.

The only major publishing venture, James Joyce's *Ulysses* (1922), almost bankrupted the store. American publishers had earlier refused the work on the grounds of explicit language and it was banned by the United States Post Office on the claim that it contained obscene material. Not only did Beach spend her personal funds to finance the publication, but she frequently "loaned" Joyce money for the family's living expenses. When Joyce sold the American publishing rights to Random House, he did not reimburse Beach for expenditures, loans, or her years of unquestioning support.

The book did help make Shakespeare and Company, as well as Beach, internationally famous. In the thirties, André Gide organized Friends of Shakespeare and Company to help with its serious financial difficulties. The committee included old friends Ernest Hemingway and T. S. Eliot and French writers Paul Valéry and Jules Romains, who not only contributed money, but gave fund-raising readings.

The occupation of France by the Germans in 1940, and the subsequent entry into the war by the United States, made Beach an enemy alien. She closed the shop in 1941, moved the books to a fourth-floor room donated by the owner of the building and, after detention in a camp in eastern France, she moved into a second-floor room. At the end of the war, she donated the library books to the American Library and moved to the larger fourth floor quarters. The shop had been leased to an antiques dealer and Beach, at fifty-eight, felt too old and tired to begin again at a new location.

During the twenties American surrealist composer George Antheil and his Hungarian-born wife lived in the two little rooms on the floor above Shakespeare and Company. With Beach's help, Antheil created a first-rate literary and music salon. Every day at 4:30 P.M. they served tea and music. He wrote of her, "To have Sylvia Beach, American ex-ambulance driver and present publisher of *Ulysses* as a landlady seemed so enormously attractive."

Not only did Beach drive an ambulance, which women were not allowed to do, but she had served as a volunteer farm worker to help the French during World War I.

Antheil's patrons included Ezra Pound and Mrs. Christian Gros, the wife of the First Secretary of the American embassy, whom he had met through Virgil Thomson. The wealthy Mrs. Gros (of the California Crocker banking family), agreed to sponsor a series of concerts by Thomson and Antheil in her luxurious Right Bank flat near the Eiffel Tower. Among the compositions played by the orchestra at the five performances was Antheil's controversial music for Fernand Léger's *Ballet Méchanique.* Eight grand pianos filled the large living room and xylophones, airplane motors, fans, an air raid siren and orchestral instruments spilled into an adjoining room and staircase. The salon was so crowded with instruments that the *bourgeoisie* and socially prominent

George Antheil, American composer, climbing the façade of
Shakespeare and Company, circa *1922 or 1923. Courtesy of*
Princeton University Library, Sylvia Beach Collection.

guests had to stand between the musicians and were even crammed into the spaces between the pianos. After surviving the loud, strange synchronizations blasting from the eclectic percussion section, there was an equally tremendous rush for the champagne. Following much imbibing, according to Antheil, the last they saw of their exquisite hostess, "she was being thrown up and down in a blanket by two princesses, a duchess, and three Italian marchesas."

Pound's pamphlet, *Antheil and the Theory of Harmony,* claimed that Antheil was the first composer to use machines. "Machines are musical . . . music is that art most fit to express the fine quality of machines."

11. Residence of Adrienne Monnier
18, rue de l' Odéon

Adrienne Monnier lived in a pleasant top floor flat until her death. Sylvia Beach shared the rooms with her from 1921 until 1932. Poetry readings were held in the book-lined living room, and Paul Valéry, André Breton and Léon-Paul Fargue often presented their works. Following the readings, cakes, sandwiches and port wine would be served.

Ernest Hemingway was among the throng when Odéonia was liberated from the Germans in 1944. Bareheaded, in shirt-sleeves, he had accompanied American and Free French soldiers as a war correspondent. He yelled "Sylvia, Sylvia," as he came down the street, until Sylvia bounded down the steps from the fifth floor and jumped into his sturdy arms. Together they drank Adrienne Monnier's wine, and then Hemingway took her next-to-last bar of soap to wash his shirt in the wash basin of his room at the Ritz Hotel.

Continue forward toward Place de l'Odéon.

12. Formerly Café Voltaire
21 Place de l' Odéon

Where the Committee for International Education-Franco-American Center now stands on the corner, once stood the Café Voltaire. The heyday of the Voltaire was the end of the Victorian period. During the Belle Epoque, Paul Gauguin, Auguste Rodin and James McNeil Whistler frequented its tables.

André Gide was among the friends and relatives of the residents of the neighborhood who could be found at the Voltaire

Robert McAlmon in Shakespeare and Company, 1923. Courtesy of Princeton University Library, Sylvia Beach Collection.

Zelda, Scottie, and Scott Fitzgerald en route *to Europe. Courtesy of Princeton University Library.*

in the first quarter of the twentieth century. Gide is considered the writer who led French literature out of the romantic and symbolist movement of the late 19th century, the prophet of individualism and castigator of social injustice. When he was eighty, in 1949, and asked what he most enjoyed in his life, Gide replied *"The Arabian Nights,* the *Bible,* the pleasures of the flesh and the Kingdom of God."

In 1957, the American cultural center, the Benjamin Franklin Library, now at Place de la Concorde near the American embassy, replaced the Voltaire. Stand on the opposite side of the Rue de l'Odéon and look for the imprint of the name plate that is still visible between the fourth and fifth windows from the corner. Directly opposite the square is an imposing structure with a facing of eight columns. The old letters *"Théâtre de l'Europe"* can be discerned on closer look.

13. Théâtre National de l' Odéon
Place de l' Odéon:

The Théâtre Français opened in 1782 with 1,913 seats. It was the grandest theater in all of Paris. The Comédie Française made it their home until 1819, and later it became the Théâtre de L'Europe. In 1959, the present name was adopted. According to French poet Paul Valéry, the Odéon was "one of the handsomest and best-sited theatres in Europe, its surroundings are sacred ground for those who prize 'Saint Language,' whether written or spoken, as one of the highest of human achievements."

On the southwest corner of the place at the intersection of Rue Regnard is the next landmark.

14. Formerly Hôtel de la Place de l'Odéon
6 Place de l'Odéon

Sisely Huddleston described Sherwood Anderson's little hotel in the shadow of the Odéon:

> *"You could hardly step out of his hotel without ascending the steps that led to the pillared arcade of the state theater, and delving into the stores of books that are exhibited along that rectangular promenade . . . They did not drive out of his mind the American scene."*

In 1921, Anderson stayed here on his first visit to Paris. The editors of *Dial* had awarded him a $2,000 prize for his contributions to American literature for his inventiveness and

Paul Valéry in Shakespeare and Company. Courtesy of Princeton University Library, Sylvia Beach Collection.

development of the modern short story form. While here, Anderson frequented the nearby Shakespeare and Company. Sylvia Beach wrote him a letter of introduction to Gertrude Stein; the meeting blossomed into a long friendship, and they corresponded for several years. In turn, Anderson introduced Hemingway to Stein. In 1921, at the age of forty-four, Anderson was already an established author and successful advertising copywriter. In a letter Stein complimented the author of *Poor White* and *Winesburg, Ohio*, "You sometimes write what is the most important thing of all to be able to write, passionate and innocent sentences."

Writer Allen Tate and his wife Caroline Gordon stayed here in 1929, and Sylvia Beach introduced them to Ernest Hemingway. Tate later wrote in *Memoirs and Opinons*:

"Ernest Hemingway was handsome and even his malice had a certain charm. I couldn't have known then that he was the complete s.o.b. who would write about certain friends all of them defenselessly dead."

Continue one block then go right on Rue de Condé and cross the street.

15. Mercure de France
26, rue de Condé

Next to the door you can still see the aging metal name plate of the Mercure de France, publishers of a leading French literary review by the same name. In 1913, Adrienne Monnier became a literary secretary at the Mercure and later she wrote, "I believe that I would have accepted sweeping the offices of the Mercure." She worked here until 1915, when her parents gave her the money that enabled her to pursue what was to be a lifelong, "beautiful heavy job."

The traditional Tuesday editorial receptions were founded by the author Mme. Rochilde, wife of Mercure founder Alfred Vallette. Distinguished men and women in art and literature attended the Mercure-sponsored banquets. In his novel, *Les Faux Monnayeurs,* André Gide describes a scene at one banquet in which one Alfred Jarry stood on a chair shooting blank cartridges at another poet. The scene really did occur at a Mercure party where Jarry took a blank shot at Christian Beck, a mutual friend of Jarry and Gide. In 1963, the Mercure published a memorial book for Sylvia Beach containing reminiscences by many of her friends.

Walk back up Rue de Condé, past the corner of Rue Regnard. Go left onto Rue Vaugirard and into Place Paul Claudel.

16. Place Paul Claudel

Diplomat, poet and playwright Paul Claudel was a close friend of Monnier, although he was often a long distance from the Odéon quarter. Claudel was the French Ambassador to Japan during most of the twenties, and from 1927 to 1933 he was the French Ambassador to the United States. In a letter to Monnier from Denmark dated 1910, Claudel claims a deep attachment to the Odéonia circle:

> *"I often think of our conversations in the Rue de l'Odéon . . . your sincerities and your enthusiasm do me good. I love gay, imaginative, and entertaining natures like your own . . . Adieu, dear Adrienne, think of me, give me the news from Paris and of all our friends and acquaintances . . ."*

Monnier sponsored two séances or meetings devoted to the readings of Claudel's poems and the production of his plays. Claudel and Monnier disagreed about the writings of James Joyce. After she published the French edition of *Ulysses,* he wrote to her:

> *"Ulysses, like the Portrait, is full of the filthiest blasphemies, in which one feels all the hatred of a renegade—afflicted moreover by a really diabolical absence of talent."*

Backtrack along Rue de Vaugirard past Rue de Condé for two blocks to the next landmark, Square Francis Poulenc.

17. Formerly Restaurant Foyot
Rue de Vaugirard and Rue de Tournon

Before the building at Number 33 was demolished, in 1933, it housed the restaurant Foyot. Booth Tarkington often ate in the popular old place, which opened in 1848. The headwaiter was the prototype for the character Amédée in *The Quest of Quernay,* in which the name of the restaurant is changed to Trois Pigeons.

18. Residence of Booth Tarkington
20 Rue de Tournon

From 1905 to 1908, Tarkington lived across the street on the sixth floor of the seven-storied building next to the post office. You can see he had a panoramic view of the city from his large windows and stone balcony. After completing *The Quest of Quernay* and leaving Paris, he wrote to a friend:

> "*Ah! The Rue de Tournon! I still haunt the neighborhood in my thoughts of Paris, but the last time I saw it was in 1911, when I went to that corner and looked up at the stone balcony that used to be mine and wondered who was living there.*"

19. Palais du Luxembourg
15, rue de Vaugirard

Directly across the Rue de Vaugirard is the drive-through entrance to the French Senate. Aunt Pauline, the small Ford truck Gertrude Stein drove from 1916 to 1918 as a volunteer for the American Fund for the French Wounded, came to a stop one day in front of the entrance. Stein, Alice B. Toklas, and Aunt Pauline were quickly surrounded by about six gendarmes. Writes Toklas, "One asked if we didn't know it was an infraction of the law to obstruct the entrance to a public building, particularly the Senate, where the prime minister is expected any minute to drive through." As the car was pushed out of the way the big black car of M. Raymond Poincaré, the French president, drove through—it had been held back by Auntie.

20. Formerly Hôtel Savoy
30, rue de Vaugirard

Upon his arrival in Paris on June 16, 1921, the young Aaron Copland lived at the Hôtel Savoy which once stood here. He then left the city to study music at Fontainebleu. At the end of the summer, Copland returned to Paris and studied with Nadia Boulanger, one of the foremost French teachers of composition. To study with a woman teacher was considered to be a rebellious act for him, and Copland wrote, "No one to my knowledge had ever thought of studying composition with a woman. Everyone knows that the world has never produced a first-rate woman composer, so it follows that no woman could possibly hope to teach composition."

As it turned out, Mme. Boulanger was a major influence on contemporary music and taught a number of Americans, including Paul Bowles, Roger Sessions, Virgil Thomson and Melville Smith. In 1924, after three years of lessons, Copland and Boulanger played a four-handed version of Virgil Thomson's ballet, *Grogh,* at the graduation party. When Boulanger toured the

United States the following year, she introduced Copland's music to his native country by playing his *Symphony for Organ and Orchestra.*

Continue up Rue Vaugirard.

21. Residence of Ford Madox Ford
Formerly 32, rue de Vaugirard

Ford Madox Ford had an apartment in the building that once stood here. Samuel Putnam, one of the few American expatriates to become part of the French community, lived nearby with his wife and son. His account of the expatriate experience, *Paris Was Our Mistress,* tells of meeting Ford on Rue de Vaugirard. Ford, an asthmatic, pushed the baby carriage through the Jardin du Luxembourg toward the Café du Dôme, all the while discoursing on Rossetti.

Ford became the mentor and publisher of short stories by Jean Rhys. Like the women in her fiction and stories, Rhys didn't fit into the aesthetic literary community of the Left Bank. She lived in the outer regions of Paris and mingled with the economically deprived and dispossessed outcasts of society, rather than in smart cafés and bookstores. Her fiction describes a sordid existence composed of tiring attempts to provide even the basic necessities of life. Ford's wife, Stella Bowen, called Rhys "a really tragic person."

In 1921, Ford left the United States for six months and loaned the apartment rent-free to Allen and Caroline Gordon Tate, and their friend, poet Lonnie Adams. Tate had received a Guggenheim grant and completed a biography of Jefferson Davis. Although he met Gertrude Stein, Alice B. Toklas, Ernest Hemingway and F. Scott Fitzgerald, Tate's Parisian experience was not particularly pleasant. His literary interest continued to be the American South and the only time a French influence appears in his work is in the 1936 publication, *The Mediterranean and Other Poems.*

22. Grand Hôtel des Principautés-Unies
42, rue de Vaugirard

Upon arrival in France in the summer of 1925, William Faulkner stayed in a top floor room. Wrote the twenty-eight-year-old to his mother, "I have a nice room just around the corner from the Luxembourg Gardens where I can sit and write and watch the children." During his six-month stay, he worked on *Mosquitoes* (1927), a satirical novel about New Orleans bohemia. Although he visited Shakespeare and Company, Faulkner made no attempt to be part of the American literary scene.

Continue up Rue Vaugirard to the corner and go right on Rue Férou.

23. Residence of Ernest and Pauline Pfeiffer Hemingway
6, rue Férou

Behind the massive gate guarded by a pair of stone sphinxes is the lavish apartment occupied in 1927 by Ernest and Pauline Pfeiffer Hemingway. The second Mrs. Hemingway had been assistant to the Paris editor of *Vogue* and a close friend of his first wife. The marriage took place in Paris in May 1927 and Ernest Hemingway wrote the World War I novel, *A Farewell to Arms,* while living here. Off a narrow entry, the living room contained a long antique oak table by a window and a large Spanish chair with a curving back. A painting by his good friend Joan Miró, which depicted a fish, decorated one wall. Miró taught Hemingway about art, and according to him before they became successful, "we were working hard but neither of us was selling anything." The Spanish painter and Hemingway met through Gertrude Stein.

24. L'Age d'Homme Publishing Co. and Former Offices of *Verve*
Rue Férou

Move down the narrow street with Ernest Hemingway to Place St.-Sulpice. On the right is the office of the publishers, L'Age d'Homme.

In the display window one might see the French edition of *Of Time and the River,* Thomas Wolfe's tale of his Paris experiences. If this were between 1937 and 1945, we would discover the office of *Verve,* the art and literary review. In its pages, co-publisher Angele Lamotte, a close friend of Adrienne Monnier, joined French society to the art and literature of the period. In 1939, they published an article by Monnier, "In the Land of Faces," about her friend Gisèle Freund.

Continue your walk down Rue Férou and make a sharp right at Place St.-Sulpice.

25. Hôtel Rècamier
3 bis, Place St.-Sulpice

In *Nightwood* (1936), Djuna Barnes describes this hotel:

"On the second landing of the hotel (it was one of those middle-class hostelries which can be found in almost any corner of Paris, neither good nor bad, but so typical that it might have been moved every night and not have been out of place) a door was standing open, exposing a red-carpeted floor, and at the further end two narrow windows overlooking the square."

Barnes had no formal education, and learned etymology by reading the *New English Dictionary*. In an introduction to her book, T. S. Eliot writes:

"What I would leave the reader prepared to find is the great achievement of a style, the beauty of phrasing, the brilliance of wit and characterization, and a quality of horror and doom very nearly related to that of Elizabethan tragedy."

Gertrude Stein and Alice Toklas frequently housed their guests in this shady, quiet corner building.

26. Place St.-Sulpice

Resting on one of the many benches in Place St.-Sulpice, with its pink flowering chestnut trees and massive fountain of four French Catholic Cardinals with royal lions at their feet, one may enjoy watching the pigeons stroll on the pavement and perch on the prelates. Gertrude Stein often passed by this area with Basket, her large white poodle. Wrote Stein, ". . . just there Basket can go free because the sidewalks are broad and not many people on them so we are often there."

Walk around the fountain, then beyond to Rue du Vieux Columbier on the west side of Place St.-Sulpice. Walk to Rue de Rennes and the St.-Sulpice Métro. Go left one block, then bear left onto Rue Cassette.

27. Residence of Alfred Jarry
7, rue Cassette

On what he termed the "third and a half floor," avant-garde poet Alfred Jarry lived from 1897 until his death on All Saints Day 1907. He named the small room *Our Grande Chasublerie (Our Large Vestment)* because a maker of religious garments occupied the second floor. Jarry's friend Henri Rousseau, described the studio as having a ceiling so low that Jarry's head collected plaster flakes quite similar to dandruff as he moved about. The only furniture was a small bed. On the wall hung a portrait of Jarry painted by Rousseau. Jarry wrote lying flat on his stomach on the floor. Known as an eccentric, Jarry led his life not only to shock society in every way possible, but to change accepted standards. Wearing a huge overcoat, Jarry carried a small library in the pockets. Because the pockets were full of holes, the books fell to the bottom of the lining. He made an amusing picture, with the swollen and heavy hem! Jarry's deep preoccupation with the subconscious mind resulted in the inseparable fusion, in the absurd, of his literary work and his behavior. His was a life experimentation.

Continue down Rue Cassette to Rue de Vaugirard and turn left.

28. Residence of F. Scott and Zelda Fitzgerald 58, rue de Vaugirard

The old stone building here with the lavishly detailed wrought-iron balconies was home to Scott and Zelda Fitzgerald for the summer of 1925. The very large apartment belonged to Gerald and Sara Murphy. "We are vaguely floating about on the surface of a fancy French apartment. It looks like the setting for one of M. Taussand's gloomier figures," wrote Zelda Fitzgerald. The sumptuously furnished major room held antique period furniture. At this time Fitzgerald was concentrating on writing short stories for publication to heal his always ailing finances. Two of the *Basil and Geraldine* stories, though based on his Midwestern childhood, were written here.

Gerald Murphy introduced Zelda Fitzgerald to the director of the ballet school for the Ballets Russes. At the age of 27, in 1927, Zelda had compulsively decided to become a ballerina and began to practice. The months in this apartment were devoted to dance lessons and long practice sessions in her attempt for instant success. The Fitzgeralds and Murphys were rich expatriates—in the case of the Fitzgeralds, they spent more money than he earned. Their group lived on the Côte d'Azur on the Mediterranean Sea for the majority of their stay in France.

Backtrack one block to Rue Madame and turn left.

29. Residence of Michael and Sarah Stein; Claribel and Etta Cone
58, rue Madame

This unusual building houses a Protestant church, as it did before when Michael and Sarah Stein and their young son Allan lived here, from 1903 to 1906, in an apartment on the upper floor. The enormous combination living-dining room had been the church assembly and Sunday school rooms. Before the present building on the west side was built, the area was lighted by large windows overlooking a garden.

The Steins admired the work of Henri Matisse and a warm friendship developed with his family. Not only did the Steins purchase a large collection of paintings and sculpture by Matisse, but in 1906, upon returning to San Francisco to examine the damage done by the earthquake and fire to their family's rental properties, they introduced the art of Matisse in the United States.

While in California, the Steins—Gertrude not among them—met Alice B. Toklas through a mutual friend, Harriet Levy. In 1907 Toklas and Levy visited Paris and called on the Steins. It was over tea here that Toklas and Gertrude Stein had their fateful first meeting and Toklas heard bells chime in her head. In Toklas' book *What is Remembered* (1963), she describes Stein, just returned from a summer in Fiosole, Italy:

"She was a golden brown presence, burned by the Tuscan sun and with a golden glint in her warm brown hair. She was dressed in a warm brown corduroy suit. She wore a large round coral brooch and when she talked, very little, or laughed, a good deal, I thought her voice came from this brooch. It was unlike anyone else's voice—deep, full, velvety like a great contralto's, like two voices. She was large and heavy with delicate small hands and a beautifully modeled and unique head."

Chimes rang for Alice B. Toklas when she met Stein because, she wrote, it was her first meeting with genius. The next two geniuses in Toklas' life were Alfred North Whitehead and Picasso. Gertrude Stein had informed her that they were geniuses.

The Cone sisters, Dr. Claribel and Etta, were Baltimore friends of Gertrude Stein when, in the fall of 1905, Etta Cone rented a flat here. Dr. Cone was furthering her medical career in Germany while her sister spent the winter reading, studying the piano, and

Sylvia Beach and Adrienne Monnier at Shakespeare and Company,
1935. Courtesy of Princeton University Library, Sylvia Beach
Collection.

visiting art galleries and museums. She also walked with young Allan Stein in the nearby Jardin du Luxembourg and joined Gertrude Stein on shopping expeditions.

While accompanying Gertrude Stein to Pablo Picasso's Montmartre studio for a sitting for the famous portrait of her, Etta Cone purchased a Picasso watercolor and an etching for twenty dollars. These were the initial purchases of what would later amount to many works by Picasso, Matisse and Paul Cézanne in the important Cone collection willed to the Baltimore Museum of Art with the provision that "the spirit of appreciation of modern art in Baltimore becomes improved." At Etta Cone's death in 1949, the collection was valued at three million dollars.

Turn right at Rue de Fleurus, cross Rue d'Assas, then turn immediately left onto Rue Duguay. Continue right onto Rue Huysmans.

30. Residence of Lily Pons
9, rue Huysmans

Soprano Lily Pons lived in a lavishly furnished eight-room apartment. At the time she was married to a wealthy patron of her musical career. Pons dressed only in *chic* black and white, changing to yellow for summer. Her dog was also yellow. Although she possessed a great deal of expensive jewelry, the couple entertained inconspicuously with only close friends.

When, in the mid-thirties, she signed a contract with the Metropolitan Opera Company and settled in New York City, the neighborhood women were surprised. They had known her only as a good Parisian housewife. Pons later divorced her French husband and in 1938 she married famed orchestra maestro André Kostelanetz.

At the end of Rue Huysmans make a right turn onto Blvd. Raspail and walk one block to Rue du Fleurus and go right.

31. Residence of Hadley Hemingway
35, rue de Fleurus

Hemingway and his first wife Hadley separated in 1926 and she took a sixth-floor apartment, no longer a part of this building, for herself, son Bumby and F. Puss Cat. Delivering her furniture and personal belongings in a rented handcart, while walking across the Jardin du Luxembourg, Hemingway burst into tears.

32. Residence of Leo Stein, Gertrude Stein, Alice B. Toklas, and Raymond Duncan
27, rue de Fleurus

The plaque on the building designates the residence of the only American commemorated by the French government. To the French, Gertrude Stein represents the pre-World War I literary community in Paris. A peek through the handsome glass gate that covers the entry, through the corridor, reveals a garden in the courtyard. Jutting out to the right of the main building is the pavillon occupied by the Steins and Toklas. The atelier is at a right angle behind the garden.

It is a Saturday evening in 1908 and we are attending a Stein soirée. Special guests such as Picasso and his current love, Fernande Olivier, have come early for dinner. Entering the pavillon through a narrow hall, one finds the small dining room through the first door on the right. Books line the walls and tacked to the doors are drawings by Picasso and Matisse. Opposite the dining room is Leo Stein's study, referred to as the *salon des refusés* because the paintings they tire of are moved here. A kitchen is in the rear. Upstairs are two bedrooms and a bath.

Exiting through the double doors in the dining room, we go outside into the atelier. The large room is furnished in handsome Italian Renaissance furniture. A stately table in the center of the room holds an inkstand and blue French school notebooks. This is where Gertrude Stein writes in the late evenings and early morning hours, at times until sunrise when the concierge extinguishes the exterior gaslight. The interior lighting is also gas. In one corner sits a large table on which lie various objects emptied from the pockets of Stein and Picasso.

At one end of the room, next to the cast iron stove, sitting in a high-back chair resembling a throne, reigns Gertrude Stein. Stein was described by Hemingway as having the head of an emperor and the body of an Irish washerwoman.

Competing for our attention are the many paintings covering the white-washed walls above the wainscotting up to the high ceiling. The sight is dazzling: works by Matisse, Picasso, Cézanne, Renoir, Gauguin, Toulouse-Lautrec, Manguin, Daumier, Delacroix and even an El Greco. Above Stein is the portrait of her painted by Picasso during the winter of 1905-1906. After eighty or ninety sittings, Picasso, in frustration, painted out the head and left for the summer in Spain. Upon his return, he completed the portrait without Stein in one afternoon. The sharp nose, straight mouth and prominent eyes of the face predicted the styles of cubism.

The many invited guests knock at the outside door of the atelier, which is then opened by Gertrude Stein. Until 1914, her brother Leo Stein also hosted the weekly parties. If this were after 1912, Alice B. Toklas would be entertaining the wives and mistresses who were seated on the other side of the room. Toklas' assigned role was to keep them occupied with women's talk of recipes, hats and fashions, and away from Stein.

In 1914, the stove was replaced by a fireplace. Electricity was installed and the passage was cut through connecting the atelier to the pavillon. Toklas moved into the study in 1912 and in 1914 Leo Stein moved permanently to Italy. The famous Stein-Toklas household was formed.

When Leo Stein moved to Paris in 1903, he studied art at the Académie Julian for, as he said to cellist Pablo Casals, he felt himself "growing into an artist." An uncle found him the apartment and atelier. The Stein family inherited money from the sale of a cable car line and from properties in San Francisco, California. The brother and sister lived comfortably on incomes of $150 a month each. This amount allowed them to travel extensively and to purchase art works for their collection of modernists. Leo Stein bought his first Cézanne, *Landscape With Spring House,* shortly after settling here. A failure at his own painting attempts, Stein was an astute judge of those artists who would become the precusors of the modernist movement: Claude Monet, Auguste Renoir, Edgar Degas and Paul Cézanne. In Gertrude Stein's words: "My brother needed to be talking and he was painting but he needed to talk about painting. He needed to understand painting in order to be painting."

The breakup of the Steins' housekeeping arrangement, in 1914, involved disagreements over the division of the art. Gertrude Stein kept the Picassos, Leo Stein the Renoirs and Matisses; they divided the Cézannes. Brother and sister disagreed strongly over the merits of Picasso whom she began patronizing in 1906 and whose works Leo Stein called "God-almighty rubbish." Upon their deaths and that of Toklas, the remaining art works were inherited by the three children of Allan Stein.

When, in 1903, Gertrude Stein moved in with her brother, she began a forty-three-year self-imposed exile from her native country. Her death in the American Hospital and burial at Père

Lachaise cemetery eternalized her expatriation. Yet she was always a loyal American, who just preferred to reside in France. Paris provided her with the peaceful environment she needed to create and she loved the French because they were friendly but not too personal.

"Paris was the place that suited those of us that were to create the twentieth-century art and literature . . . France could be civilized without having progress on her mind, she could believe in civilization in and for itself, and so she was the natural background for this period."

Stein never spoke French fluently, preferring to speak in the language of her writing. When the Americans came to France in both World Wars, Toklas and she proudly greeted the servicemen. Upon returning from an American tour in 1932-33, she exclaimed, "I am already homesick for America. I never knew it was so beautiful. I was like a bachelor who goes along fine for twenty-five years and then decides to get married. This is the way I feel—I mean about America."

Sitting on the high Renaissance chair or walking the streets of Paris, Stein was usually dressed in a long brown skirt, a fancy vest and handmade Italian sandals. She looked patriarchal, but also appeared shy at times—but not about her talents. Immodest Stein left some memorable assertions, such as, "Einstein was the creative philosophical mind of the century and I have been the creative literary mind of the century."

Stein wrote essays, plays, short stories, novels, word portraits and an opera. Virgil Thomson declared: "To have become a Founding Father of her generation is her reward for having long ago completely dominated her language." She always wrote about realities—the people she knew, the places, objects and events around her. She experimented with novel forms of style and punctuation. Many Americans who have never read any of her works are familiar with the repetitive sentence, "A rose is a rose is a rose," and have heard "Pigeons on the grass, alas." Residents of Oakland, California, scene of her childhood, have never forgiven Stein for her description of their city—"There is no there, there." A banner waving the word "there" now flies above the Oakland City Hall.

It is here that Toklas was secretary, housekeeper, cook, gardener, companion and loyal supporter to Stein. For nearly 40 years she submerged her public personality to that of the more flamboyant Stein. In private, however, Toklas was the strength and rock that the "genius" needed in order to act on her creative urges. The daily pressures were relieved by Toklas and no writer ever had a more admiring public of one.

They made a striking, if unusual couple. Toklas, small, thin and dark, dressed in flowery gowns and unusual, slightly unflattering hats. She frequently screened callers and protected Stein. In the *Alice B. Toklas Cookbook* are her favorite recipes which she cooked with ingredients grown in the garden of Billignin, their summer residence in eastern France.

After her beloved Gertrude died in 1946, Toklas wrote the charming account of their years together, and of the many celebrities involved in their lives. She writes poignantly in *What is Remembered*, "It was Gertrude Stein who held my complete attention, as she did for all the many years I knew her until her death, and all these many empty ones since."

Around 1905 Raymond Duncan, brother of dancer Isadora Duncan, lived in a studio in this building. The Stein family were old friends from San Francisco. Accompanied by a Greek girlfriend and dressed in Greek robes, he had just returned from Greece. Since he was penniless, Gertrude Stein gave him coal for his stove and a chair and Duncan used packing cases for the rest of the furniture.

When a son was born to Penelope, Duncan and Michael Stein registered the birth. They named him Raymond because a name had not been chosen. Later it was changed to the Greek name Menolka.

Continue along the Rue de Fleurus and through the tall gold-topped fence of the Jardin du Luxembourg.

33. Jardin du Luxembourg

At their first meeting, Gertrude Stein invited Alice B. Toklas to accompany her on a walk the next day. The walks continued for their time together. Leaving the Rue de Fleurus, we join them as they stroll through the Jardin du Luxembourg toward the rear of the palace and the Medici Fountain, then exit at Place Edmond Rosland. They continue down the Blvd. St-Michel, stopping at a pastry shop. There they eat a praline ice, "just like that in San Francisco."

Walking with his small son Bumby or going to visit Gertrude Stein, Hemingway frequently crossed these gardens. In *Islands in the Stream,* he notes:

"I can remember the Jardin du Luxembourg well. I can remember afternoons with the boats on the lake by the fountain in the big garden with the trees. The paths through the trees were all gravelled and the men played bowling games off to the left under the trees as we went down toward the palace. In the fall, the leaves came down and I can remember the trees bare on the gravel. I like to remember the fall best . . . the way the gravel was dry on top when everything was damp and the wind in the trees that brought the leaves down."

In these gardens Henry Miller and Alfred Perlès would enjoy lunch together. They brought a picnic—cheese and ham, a bunch of bananas and a couple of bottles of wine. Sitting on a bench facing the statues of the queens of France and Navarre, they consumed the food and drank the wine straight from the bottles.

The bronze statue "Russian Bacchanale" by Malvina Hoffman was placed in the gardens in 1917. During World War II, it was melted down by the German occupiers of Paris and made into enemy shells.

Exit the garden on the south side at Rue Auguste-Comte. Turn left and continue to Blvd. St.-Michel.

34. Foyer International des Etudiantes
93, blvd. St.-Michel

This is still the site of the Foyer International des Etudiantes, as it was in 1942 when Sylvia Beach began staying here at times during the war years. Beach felt unsafe in her apartment on Rue de l'Odéon, and she often hid in a top floor studio with a small kitchen away from the Germans.

Walk north along Blvd. St.-Michel and return to the garden. Continue through the statuary past the fountains and trees, past the Palace, and through the northeast gate onto Rue de Vaugirard; then continue to the museum.

35. Musée du Luxembourg

The Musée du Luxembourg was the primary source of late nineteenth and early twentieth century art collections that are now exhibited in the new Musée d'Orsay. Founded in 1818 by

Louis XVIII to house the paintings and sculptures of the modern school, the museum contained the only state-owned works of art by living artists. During the 1870s and 1880s the Luxembourg was opposed to vanguard ideas in art, but in 1890 a group of subscribers organized by Claude Monet purchased Manet's *Olympia* and donated it to the state. In 1896 the impressionists were fully accepted by the museum, which now presented a strong showing of impressionist works: seven pastels by Degas, two Manets, two Cézannes, eight Monets, six Renoirs, six Sisleys, and seven Pisarros. In 1922 the Jeu de Paume museum of the Louvre opened, and impressionists were officially accepted by the State when their works were gathered there in 1929.

Many modern artists of the Left Bank offered their works to the French government as gifts to be hung in the museum, but the gesture was refused. The Musée du Luxembourg was dissolved in 1937 and replaced by the Musée Nationale d'Art Moderne. By then it took a fortune for the new state museum to acquire the same paintings that previously were offered as gifts.

The Luxembourg is now open for special exhibits. One can find many attractive posters announcing the current show throughout the neighborhood.

WALK

THE

ARTISANS AND

FOUNDRIES

FOUR

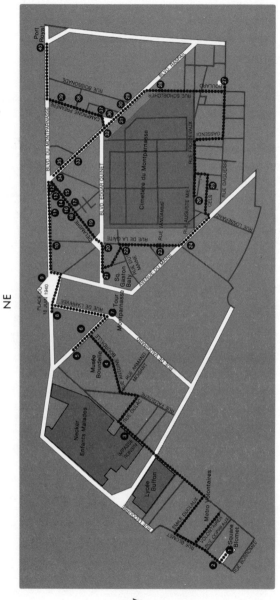

WALK IV

Métro: Volontaires; Bus: 39

If you arrived by train at the Volontaires Métro station, upon exiting turn right on Rue des Volontaires and proceed to Rue Blomet. You can feel how the ambiance of this working class quarter is unchanged from the latter part of the nineteenth century and the early years of the twentieth, when large spaces were available for low rent and the neighborhood consisted of minor artisans and metal foundries. According to Paul Valéry, French sculpture in the eighteenth and nineteenth centuries had asserted itself as the "foremost in the world."

Turn left and walk one long block to Square Blomet.

1. Rue Blomet Group
Square Blomet and 45, rue Blomet

Through the metal entrance gates of the park, in the rear next to the children's playground, rests a large sculpture by Joan Miró. French children play in the shadow of its smooth metal protuberances, unaware that in the 1920s this was home to the Rue Blomet Group of surrealist artists.

In warm weather, dada artists André Masson, Francis Picabia and Antonin Artaud, among others, would gather around a single lilac tree in the courtyard arguing wildly with dada cofounder Tristran Tzara. Cubism had been the major modern art movement, but Tzara announced that cubism was now dead. The Rue Blomet Group joined the surrealists led by André Breton.

Spanish artist Joan Miró followed fellow Catalanian Pablo Picasso to Paris from Barcelona. Picasso found him a room in an inexpensive hotel on the Right Bank, but when Miró decided to settle permanently in Paris, he established his studio-home here in a building about to collapse. The fastidious Miró whitewashed the walls of his room and kept his paints, brushes and canvases neatly arranged. In order to create, he needed organization in his surroundings.

The large painting, *The Farm (1922),* purchased by Miró's friend Hemingway, represents the crisp, ornate realism of his works when he first moved here. In about 1926, his style simplified to demonstrate his wit and childlike sense of the fun in life. He joined the surrealists in seeking "a kind of absolute reality, a super-reality."

Next door to Miró's clean space the artist André Masson lived in exactly opposite conditions. A true bohemian, he was inspired

Sculpture by Joan Miró, 45, rue Blomet. Courtesy of Felicity Leng.

Sculpture dedicated to Apollinaire, by Picasso. Courtesy of Felicity Leng.

by squalor. He agreed with Philippe Soupault, who once exclaimed, "Cleanliness is the luxury of the poor—be dirty!" Masson's works are very abstract, with no discernible form, in which the emotions of the creator dominate.

"For us, surrealists of 1924, the great prostitute was reason," Masson wrote. "It was cool reason, after all, that led mankind into the war to end all wars." In rainy weather, fellow surrealists Soupault, Francis Picabia, Tristan Tzara and Emil Artaud would forsake the ambiance of the lilac tree to meet in Masson's disordered studio.

2. Formerly Le Bal Nègre
46, rue Blomet

When Josephine Baker introduced American jazz to Paris, the French loved the rhythms. The Charleston dance was an immediate hit. It was no longer considered *chic* to attend the neighborhood *bals musette*. The Americans now thronged to trendy, swinging black cabarets such as this.

It was at the Bal Nègre that *transition* editor Eugene Jolas introduced writer Kay Boyle to his wealthy new friends, Harry and Caresse Crosby. The Crosby's Black Sun Press was to publish Boyle's first book, *Short Stories* (1929), a group of seven short stories, all but one of which had been printed previously in various small magazines.

Walk back up Blomet three blocks and turn right onto Rue Emile-Duclaux, which will return you to Rue de Vaugirard. Turn left and walk about five blocks. Next to Number 164 on Rue de Vaugirard is an old building that looks as if it could hold a sculptor's studio. The impasse next door is unmarked.

3. Studio of Constantin Brancusi
8, Impasse Ronsin

Beyond the large metal gates, opening on a courtyard, was the studio of sculptor Constantin Brancusi. The white-walled room on the ground floor had high, raftered walls. Work benches were strewn with chisels. Saws hung from pegs on the walls. Wood shavings and stone dust from the white and silver statues covered the floor.

Brancusi often cooked and entertained, telling many dramatic stories. With his dark piercing eyes, pink cheeks and long white beard, he would laugh loudly, often gesticulating widely with his arms and dancing while narrating the tales. The Crosbys had lunch in the studio and watched Brancusi roast chicken and potatoes in the open fireplace that also served as his sculptor's forge. Anaïs Nin reported being served shish-kebab and large bottles of red wine.

When attending the local cinema Brancusi's large Spitz dog Polaris sat in the previously reserved seat next to his master. Presumably he also loved films.

For two years, from 1926 to 1928, the United States Custom Service argued with Brancusi over his modern piece of sculpture, *l'Oiseau d'Or*. They declared the highly polished piece of metal to be a piece of "detached metal" rather than a work of art and thus eligible for a higher import duty. In court the U.S. government conceded that the piece of sculpture did possess qualities of "an ornamental nature" and would not be classified as raw metal. The outcome of the lawsuit proscribed the judgment officials could make when confronted with examples of modern art. Brancusi referred to his stone, wood and metal works as "sculpture for the blind" because the figures and objects were so simplified they could be understood by touch.

Proceed along Rue de Vaugirard to the first corner, Rue Dulac, and turn right. At Rue Falguière turn left, and after one short block bear right at Rue Antoine Bourdelle.

4. Musée Bourdelle
16, rue Antoine Bourdelle

Behind the surrounding fence, the front garden filled with large stone figures will immediately catch your attention. Inside the buildings is a large collection of Antoine Bourdelle's work and the rooms where he lived. This little-publicized museum is a jewel for art lovers.

Bourdelle lived here from 1881 to 1929. The street had been opened in 1913 and in 1935, after Bourdelle's death, it was named for him.

Commenting on his beloved teacher Auguste Rodin, Bourdelle said: "I was only the workman." He felt Rodin was the genius; he only continued his work. In the twenties, American sculptor Jo Davidson rented space here to cut his large stones. His atelier was nearby.

Another American sculptor, Frederick William MacMonnies, kept his studio at this address. Janet Scudder saw his famous fountain for the Court of Honor at the World's Columbian Exposition in 1893 and, in 1894, she became MacMonnie's assistant. She helped him chisel *Victory* for the battle monument at West Point and *Bacchante* for Jardin du Luxembourg.

Continue toward the intersection and turn left on Avenue du Maine.

5. Residence of Kahlil Gibran
14, Avenue du Maine

Widely read poet, artist and philosopher Kahlil Gibran lived here from 1908 to 1910, and during this time he wrote in Arabic. When he settled in America, in 1911, he switched to the English language. Although best known in the United States for his mystical works such as *The Prophet* (1923), while living in Paris, Rodin commissioned him to paint his portrait.

Upon his death on 10 April 1931, Gibran's will stipulated that all royalties from his work would go to his birthplace, Bechari, Lebanon. With the renewal of the copyrights of some of his books, his sister made claim to some of the royalties. During the time the court took to review the matter, Gibran's American publisher Alfred Knopf did not distribute any money and the profits kept piling up. Eventually, the enormous sum was divided between the town and his sister.

Cross Avenue du Maine and walk to the right.

6. Studio of Jo Davidson
21, Avenue du Maine

Walk to the rear of the impasse of old colorful buildings.

Sculptor Jo Davidson lived here at Number 14, for ten years in a studio with a southern exposure consisting of two rooms and a large balcony. Here, often in quick four or five hour single settings, he modeled busts of such diverse subjects as Andrew Mellon, Clarence Darrow, Bernard Baruch, Charles Chaplin, Gandhi, and James Joyce.

In 1923, when he posed Gertrude Stein, raised on a small platform, her shoulders hunched forward and her hands resting in her spacious lap, he wrote:

"To do a head of Gertrude was not enough—there was so much more of her than that. So I did a seated figure of her—a sort of modern Buddha . . . she would come around to my studio and read aloud. The extraordinary part of it was that, as she

Gertrude Stein, by Jo Davidson. Courtesy of Research Library, Department of Special Collections, University of California— Los Angeles.

read, I never felt any sense of mystification. 'A rose is a rose
is a rose,' took on a different meaning with each inflection.
When she read aloud, I got the humor of it. We both laughed,
and her laughter was something to hear. There was an eter-
nal quality about her—she somehow symbolized wisdom."

The word portrait of Davidson Stein composed while she
posed was published in *Vanity Fair* along with a photograph of
the sculpture.

It was also in this studio that Gertrude Stein and James Joyce
first met, at a tea party Davidson gave in celebration of the completion of his statue of Walt Whitman. Sylvia Beach did the
introduction, and Stein later recalled that she had said, "we have
never met and he said no although our names are always together,
and then we talked of Paris and where we lived and why we lived
where we lived and that was all . . ."

7. Formerly Palais d'Orléans
Avenue du Maine

Too far down Avenue du Maine for this walk is the site of
the former Palais d'Orléans, where a banquet honoring Apollinaire was held on December 31, 1916. In the same dining room
that was the scene of a banquet for Paul Verlaine twenty-five years
earlier, Apollinaire's friends welcomed him back to Paris after
a severe head injury he had suffered in the war. The organizers
of the grand affair were Juan Gris, Pablo Picasso, Paul Dermee,
Max Jacob and Blaise Cendrars. Ninety guests attempted to con-
sume a twelve-course meal. The printed menu listed *"Hors
d'oevres Cubistes, Orphistes Futuristes, Méditations Esthétiques
en Salade, Café des Soirées de Paris"*, and many bottles of
"alcools," in honor of Apollinaire's collection of poems by that
name.

A brawl developed between rival groups of cubists. Apollinaire, smartly dressed in a new uniform, quieted the raucus
guests with a recitation and a toast. He later wrote: "My dinner
was a sort of magnesium flash, exactly what it should have been,
explosive and dangerous, brief, but carried to the verge of
paroxysm."

Continue down Avenue du Maine to the corner, then take
a sharp left at the corner onto Rue de l'Arrivée and continue up
to the very busy Blvd. du Montparnasse. The controversial, bold
black Tour Montparnasse will be on your right. At the corner,

turn left. The tower is the only skyscraper in central Paris and the shopping center from which it soars is the first of its kind to be seen by Parisians from most Left Bank locations. Since it is taller than the Eiffel Tower, most Frenchmen consider it to be an ugly blight in the city's panorama.

8. Formerly Hôtel de Versailles
60, blvd. du Montparnasse

Alexander Calder stayed here for four months when he first arrived in France in July 1926. He had come to paint. Later, when told his art was really American, Calder replied: "I got the impulse for doing things my way in Paris."

Turn around and walk back along Blvd. du Montparnasse crossing Rue de l'Arrivée and continue past the shopping center to the Montparnasse Metro station. From here, look across Place du 18 Juin 1940. (To cross it is to take your life in your hands.)

9. Formerly Restaurant Trianon
5, Place du 18 Juin 1940

Formerly named Place de Rennes, Number Five was the favorite restaurant of James Joyce. The nearly blind author always sat at a reserved table with his frequent dinner companions John Dos Passos and Samuel Beckett. Joyce, very thin, usually wore a flower-embroidered vest, with a large ring bejeweling his little finger. He wore very thick glasses. The waiter usually read the menu to him.

When Robert McAlmon hosted a party for poet William Carlos Williams, the large literary crowd almost filled the left side of the restaurant. Joyce, after too much to drink, sang Irish ballads. McAlmon sang Negro spirituals and cowboy songs.

At this time Williams had growing discomfort and doubts about expatriation to Europe. He was on a sabbatical from his medical practice in Rutherford, New Jersey, and soon made the decision to return to America.

Continue along the crowded sidewalk and turn right at the next street, Rue du Montparnasse.

10. Café Falstaff
42, rue du Montparnasse

When Jimmy the Barman (Jimmy Chaters) left the Dingo Bar, his many literary customers followed. The Falstaff, with oak panelled walls and padded chair seats, was more attractive and quiet and today its ambiance is the same as it was nearly sixty years ago.

In the summer of 1929, Morley Callaghan walked into Jimmy's with Ernest Hemingway and F. Scott Fitzgerald. "I laughed and said that by tomorrow word would go around the cafe that I, shamelessly, was telling Fitzgerald and Hemingway what to do with a book. Ernest said: 'What do you care? We're professionals. We only care whether a thing is as good as it should be.' "

Back on the boulevard, continue to your right again.

11. La Coupole
Blvd. du Montparnasse and Rue Vavin

Before the Russian Revolution, Leon Trotsky and fellow exiles met here to design socialist doctrine. After the revolution, it was the White Russian emigrées who sat here reading the Russian language newspapers always found on the racks. Paris always welcomed the Russians in the arts. Diaghilev, the impressario of the Ballets Russes, and musicians Sergei Prokoviev and Igor Stravinsky made their home here. Paris life stimulated Stravinsky so much that he became a French citizen. Prokofiev resisted becoming Parisian. "To settle in Paris does not mean that one immediately becomes Parisian," he stated. His music continued to be purely Slavic in style.

12. Café du Dôme
108, blvd. du Montparnasse

In a letter to Sherwood Anderson, dated December 23, 1921, Ernest Hemingway wrote: ". . . we sat outside the Dôme opposite the Rotonde that's being redecorated, warmed up against one of those charcoal braziers and it's damned cold outside and the braziers make it so warm."

Originally a seedy neighborhood bar started by two brothers, the Dôme became a Montparnasse hangout for American painters and expatriate writers. Americans went there to see who was having breakfast with whom, or who was invited to sit at whose table. It was a living newspaper. Malcolm Cowley wrote that the editors of little magazines patronized the Dôme in search of contributors. It was easier than writing letters.

At the corner of Place Pablo Picasso, turn a sharp right onto Rue Delambre.

13. Formerly Black Manikin Press and Residence of Edward Titus
4, rue Delambre

Around the corner from the Dôme, Edward Titus, first husband of Helena Rubenstein, opened the Sign of the Black Manikin bookstore in 1924. His Black Manikin Press, begun in 1926, published the second edition of D. H. Lawrence's *Lady Chatterly's Lover* among the twenty-five volumes printed here through 1932. He edited *This Quarter* from 1921 until its demise three years later.

Titus lived above the shop in an elegant apartment furnished with antiques paid for, but rarely visited, by Mme. Rubenstein, who considered their bi-continental arrangement the modern way of marriage. She did not approve of his friends, Joyce, Lawrence, Hemingway, Faulkner and e.e. cummings, thinking them "wasters" for whose meals she was always paying.

14. Residence of Samuel and Riva Putman
8, rue Delambre

Practically above the Dingo Bar and in back of the Coupole lived writers Samuel and Riva Putnam. In 1930, Putnam was the associate editor of *This Quarter*. In the cramped little apartment of two small, joined rooms they once had a Vodka party for playwright Elmer Rice and no fewer than a hundred guests crowded into the tiny space. Putnam wrote that the kitchen of the Coupole "used to provide us with an orchestrated accompaniment of rattling dishes."

15. Residence of Isadora Duncan
9, rue Delambre

Directly across the street is a glass-front building that was completed in 1926, the year Isadora Duncan moved into a cramped duplex apartment inside. On one floor was her studio with a bedroom and bathroom above, and a small balcony overlooked the studio below. This was her final home in Paris before she died in Nice the following year, strangled in her own luxurious, trailing scarf that had caught in the wheels of the convertible in which she was riding.

By her account Duncan was so poor at this time that she hardly knew where her next bottle of champagne was coming from. In hopes that book sales would be the means of improving her impoverished life, she continued to write her memoirs. Unfortunately, *My Life* was published posthumously.

In her younger days Duncan was paid huge sums for a single performance. She lived extravagantly, spent numerous fortunes and was generous with her many friends. During the First World War, she donated Belleville, her Paris chateau, to the French government to be used as a hospital. When Duncan rented the Metropolitan Opera House in New York City for a fundraising performance, she danced for free, the proceeds being donated to France.

16. Formerly Dingo Bar
10, rue Delambre

Jimmy the Barman's corned beef, beefsteak, American soup, and friendliness drew scores of Americans here. Upon first meeting F. Scott Fitzgerald at the Dingo, Hemingway described him as:

". . . a man who looked like a boy with a face between handsome and pretty [with fair hair and a] delicate long-lipped Irish mouth . . . the mouth worried you until you knew him, then it worried you more."

Their future friendship was based more on common literary interests than personal attraction. Although he especially admired Hemingway, the Fitzgeralds' inability to hold liquor and their other extravagant excesses bothered him. Fitzgerald, who emulated and wrote about the rich, once said to Hemingway, "The rich are not as we are." Hemingway answered, "No, they have more money."

17. Formerly Hôtel des Ecoles
15, rue Delambre

From November 1921 to the summer of 1922, when Man Ray was struggling to be a modern painter, he lived here on the same floor as Tristan Tzara. Soon after Man Ray discovered his true expression in photography and became successful.

The Rumanian artist, Tzara was the philosophical founder of the dada movement in Zurich, and his arrival in Paris was a great moment in the twentieth century to many artists who had long awaited him. Dada art was a negative reaction to current ideological and aesthetic preconceptions which led to political upheaval and suffering. Wars are senseless, therefore art makes no sense, reasoned the dadaists. They aimed to shock people in an effort to show the insanity of life and the worthlessness of Western mores. Dadaism by 1923 evolved into surrealism.

18. Residence of Frederick MacMonnies
22, rue Delambre

Sculptor Frederick MacMonnies came to Paris to study at the Ecole des Beaux-Arts. He lived here and maintained his studio on the Rue Antoine Bourdelle where Janet Scudder worked as his assistant.

Continue past Square Delambre.

19. Residence of Jo Davidson
39, rue Delambre

While an art student in 1908, Jo Davidson lived in a ground floor studio. A very talented sculptor, he could work very quickly, sometimes creating a bust in a single two-hour sitting. When he heard that some American students were looking for a bust of Wagner to present to their teacher, Davidson claimed he had one. Borrowing twenty francs to purchase a photo of the composer, he completed the sculpture in twenty-four hours. When asked how long he worked on it, he replied, "Oh, a couple of months."

Davidson's subjects included Marshal Foch of France, General George Pershing, Bernard Baruch, and John D. Rockefeller. He was relatively unknown until he sold his first piece to Mrs. Harry Payne Whitney (*née* Gertrude Vanderbilt), the founder of the Whitney Museum of American Art in New York. Through her he gained a reputation among important buyers in New York and Paris.

Cross Blvd. Edgar Quinet and onto Rue de la Gaité.

20. Residence of Raymond and Isadora Duncan
4, rue de la Gaité

Raymond Duncan arrived in Paris in 1900, and was joined by his mother and sister Isadora. They settled in a furnished studio in a courtyard, which rented for fifty francs a month. The concierge provided lunch for twenty-five *centimes,* and dinner, including wine, cost one franc per person.

The brother and sister would spend their days in the Louvre; she in a white dress and "Liberty of London" hat, he with long hair topped by a black hat and open collar and flowing tie, in imitation of the Latin Quarter artists.

After six months the family moved to larger quarters over a printing press that worked around the clock and made the building shake.

Much later, in January 1927, Isadora Duncan was the subject of Janet Flanner's first profile in the *New Yorker:* "Two decades before (1907) her art, animated by her extraordinary personality, came as close to founding an aesthetic renaissance as American morality would allow."

Return to Blvd. Edgar Quinet and turn left, walking north.

21. Formerly Le Sphinx
31, blvd. Edgar Quinet

The bygone stucco building was replaced by this ordinary modern one. Enhancing the sober cemetery neighborhood, Le Sphinx, a *maison de joie* or bordello, was easily identified by the two stone sphinxes that guarded the entrance. For its grand opening, Mme. Martha Lemestre distributed elegant invitations to all the men in the neighborhood, many of whom attended with their wives. They found art deco, Egyptian-style furnishings, hostesses reputed to be exceptionally attractive and charming, and superb wines from the well-stocked cellar.

To make the important guests comfortable in summer, Le Sphinx was air-conditioned. It was the first building in France with this luxury.

Backtracking down Edgar Quinet again, turn right onto Rue Poinsot and walk across Square Gaston-Baty to Rue du Maine.

22. Hôtel Central
1 bis, rue du Maine

Overlooking the little square formed by seven mangy trees enclosing a few wooden benches, the hotel sits on the corner. In 1930 Henry Miller and Alfred Perlès occupied adjoining rooms. At the time Perlès wrote for the Paris *Tribune.* Miller was unemployed and almost as destitute as the beggars and sandwichmen of the quarter, who ate their bread and cheese lunches in the square, drinking *vin ordinaire* straight from the bottle. The job

Perlès found him at the *Tribune* lasted only a few months. Miller claimed he came to Paris to study sin.

At the corner turn right onto Rue de la Gaité. The next landmark will be on the left.

23. Formerly Théâtre de la Gaité
26, rue de la Gaité

Isadora Duncan's greatest triumph, on January 27, 1909, was her performance of *Iphegenie* by Christoph von Gluck. The critic of the Paris newspaper *L'Opinion* wrote that she danced with "exquisite grace, fine elegance and lightness. Most of all, she gives the illusion of the most perfect naturalness." In bare feet and a sheer Grecian robe, Duncan initiated a new school of dance. Soon groups of young American women were floating free-style and ungirdled in performances held in gardens and Greek amphitheaters.

Follow Rue de la Gaité to Avenue du Maine.

24. Residence of Henri Rousseau
Formerly 2 bis, rue Perrel

Across Avenue du Maine, where a high-rise development now stands, on a short impasse that no longer exists, Henri Rousseau lived in a single room over a plasterer's shop. To paint full-time, he retired at forty from the French civil service after years spent as a weekend artist. The nickname, *Le Douanier,* persisted long after Rousseau quit his post as a customs officer. Rousseau commented that he did not mind living in one small room because every morning when he awoke he could "smile a little at his paintings."

Before two of his works were accepted for the 1905 Salon d'Automne, Rousseau was as poor as his neighbors. He would walk all over Paris, his violin under his arm, to give music lessons. He later opened a school in his studio to pay for his paint and canvases. Over the doorway to the studio a sign said, "Courses in Diction, Music, Painting Solfeggio." Rousseau charged eight francs a month for lessons. After his success at the Salon, he was accepted by other avant-garde artists such as Henri Matisse, Georges Braque, Georges Rouault and Raoul Dufy, and dealers began to buy his paintings.

In about 1907, Rousseau began hosting Saturday parties and in the following years his friends, students, and neighbors would anticipate the arrival of Rousseau's formal invitations. Meanwhile the room would be carefully arranged. Rousseau would clean up the studio floor and cover it with a rug that he had traded three paintings to acquire. The bed was then folded and tucked into a corner, and bottles of wine would be lined up on the table. Rousseau, like a formal butler, met the guests at the door and ushered them to their seats in the order of their arrival. The chairs were arranged to face a makeshift stage. The guests were invited to perform; there was much drinking and laughter, and Rousseau often played a flute while dancing and giggling.

Well-known Parisians who participated in the supposedly literary soirées included Apollinaire, Picasso, Braque, Jacob, Brancusi and Jules Romains.

Max Weber wrote of Rousseau, "Here is a man, an artist, a poet, whose friendship and advice I must cultivate and cherish."

Continue along Avenue du Maine, past Rue Froidevaux. Your next left will be the tiny Rue Auguste Mie, then bear immediately right onto Rue Cels.

25. Studio of Alexander Calder
7, rue Cels

Working in a ground-floor studio in January 1927, Alexander Calder produced his miniature circus, to the delight of his friends Léger, Miró, and Jean Cocteau. Calder unrolled a strip of green carpet, laid out the miniature ring and manipulated marionettes of trained dogs, acrobats, trapeze artists and tumblers. The circus is on permanent display in the Whitney Museum, New York City.

Proceed down Rue Cels, turn left on Rue Fermat and go one block, then left again onto Rue Froideveaux. The Cimitière du Montparnasse is on the right. The old cemetery of 1824 contains the graves of sculptors Frederic Auguste Bertholdi (Statue of Liberty), Henri Laurens and Brancusi. Impressionist painter Henri Fantin and expressionist Chaim Soutain rest here. The hearse of existentialist Jean-Paul Sartre, who lived nearby on the Blvd. Raspail with writer Simone de Beauvoir, was followed by 50,000 mourners. Dadaist Tristan Tzara, reader of the telephone book as poetry, lies here under a plain marker.

26. Studio of Gerald Murphy
69, rue Froidevaux

The third building from the corner is unusual for Paris, where one rarely finds brick buildings. Built in the Second Empire reign of Francis I, (1515-1547), it once held the simple studio of Gerald

Murphy. In an attempt to escape from joining the family leather business, Mark Cross, Murphy intended to study landscape engineering in Paris. Upon viewing cubist paintings he exclaimed, "If that's painting, it's what I want to do." Fernand Léger strongly influenced his style and considered him to be the only American artist of any importance. Murphy's large paintings of 1925 were executed in the flat colors of posters. Critics didn't consider them to be art, but rather architectural drawings. Because he felt his work would never be accepted as first rate, "and the world is too full of second-rate painting," after the mid-twenties Murphy never painted again.

When Ernest and Hadley Hemingway separated in August 1926, Murphy loaned him the use of the studio, furnished only with a bed and a table. Here Hemingway completed correcting proofs of *The Sun Also Rises.*

About-face, and walk to the fourth corner before you turn right. Then left at the first street, Rue Daguerre.

27. Residence of Alexander Calder
22, rue Daguerre

During the winter of 1926, Alexander Calder lived in a rear second-floor apartment here. Instead of painting he created small unusual wire figures. The suggestion for them had come from W. C. Williams. One of his first models was a wire figure of Josephine Baker. A number of other pieces dangled freely from string attachments, and because of their movements Calder's friend Marcel Duchamp coined the name "mobiles." This novel form of art won Calder international fame.

Backtrack up Daguerre and take a right on Rue Boulard, which in two blocks becomes Rue Schoelcher.

28. Residence of Pablo Picasso
5 bis, rue Schoelcher

Describing a 1914 walk down the Blvd. Raspail on a cold winter evening with Picasso, his mistress Eve (Marcelle Humbert), and Toklas, Gertrude Stein wrote, "There is nothing in the world colder than the Raspail on a cold winter evening, we used to call it the retreat from Moscow." Down the street came a cannon painted in camouflage, the first they had seen. "It is we that created that," said Picasso, referring also to the landscapes of

Cézanne and himself that blended buildings into the surrounding country and were the initial cubist paintings.

Stein believed that the landscapes Picasso painted on summer trips to Spain were the beginning of cubism. The treatment of the houses, not following the landscape, but rather cutting across and into it, thereby making the houses indistinguishable from the countryside, was essentially Spanish. The colors of his landscapes were Spanish—pale silver yellow with a hint of green. According to Stein, "Cubism is a purely Spanish conception and only Spaniards can be cubists."

From 1913 to 1916, when he lived here, Picasso painted in the brilliant colors and the variety of painted textures of abstract imagery. In 1915, he reverted to a realistic execution of drawings and portraits. Said Picasso, "Everytime I begin a picture, I feel as though I were throwing myself into the void."

Turn left at Blvd. Raspail and walk one block. The next two landmarks will be across the street.

29. Residence of Mariette Mills
Rue Boissonade

Sculptor Mariette Mills lived in a beautiful studio somewhere on the street. Wrote Robert McAlmon, "When Picabia, Léger, Brancusi, Mina Loy and Duchamp were there for dinner, there was brighter and more intelligent conversation than one was apt to get elsewhere in Paris."

30. Residence of Mildred Aldrich
Rue Boissonade and Blvd. Raspail

Mildred Aldrich lived in a corner building on the top floor from the early 1900s until she moved to a village a few hours away from Paris in 1914. She was retired from a long career as an editor and critic of the theater and cultural events for papers in New England. Aldrich chose to live out her life in France because she considered America to be "the land of the young, the energetic, and the ambitious, the ideal home of the very rich and the laboring classes."

From the time Gertrude Stein settled in Paris in 1903, she and Aldrich were close friends. Like Alice B. Toklas, she believed that anything Stein said or did was worthwhile. Her move to the Marne Valley, when living in Paris became too expensive, resulted in the publication in 1915 in America of her popular book

Hilltop on the Marne, a description of her view of the Battle of the Marne of September 1914. From her small cottage that overlooked the Marne river she watched the bloody battle, and then helped care for the wounded.

Cross to the left side of Blvd. Raspail again.

31. Residence of Pablo Picasso
242 blvd. Raspail

Before moving to Rue Schoelcher in 1912, Picasso first moved here from Montmartre. As the rents increased in the northern bucolic butte, the artists moved south across the Seine to Montparnasse, which consequently became the center for modern painters. By this time, Picasso was a regular visitor to Gertrude Stein's pavillon. Alice B. Toklas described him as "very dark with black hair, a lock hanging over one of his marvelous all-seeing black eyes."

By 1908, Picasso and Braque had pushed the frontiers of art with cubism. They pasted calling cards, bits of newsprint, chair caning and pieces of rope on the canvases—the first collages. When Gertrude Stein left her calling card, after paying him a visit and finding him out, he glued the card on a painting.

32. Formerly Gypsy Bar
Blvd. Raspail and Blvd. Edgar Quinet

In the spring of 1921, Joyce, McAlmon, and British author Wyndham Lewis met nightly at the Gypsy Bar, sometimes staying until dawn. After a few drinks, Joyce would recite his own works or long passages from Dante in Italian. Lewis would occasionally deliver readings from the works of Verlaine.

33. Formerly Theater of Edward Titus
216, blvd. Raspail

Built by Edward Titus in 1921, the apartment house held his "little American theater" of three hundred seats. Financed by his wife, Helena Rubenstein, Titus produced only avant-garde productions in French, English and Italian. The performances were strictly for invited audiences, but the French government shut the theater down on the grounds that the plays attacked the French state.

34. Hôtel Raspail
Blvd. Raspail and Rue Delambre

When Samuel and Riva Putnam and their eight-month-old son Hilary first arrived in Paris in the fall of 1926, they stayed here. Putnam was writing a Paris art letter for the *Chicago Daily News.* It was to Putnam that Gertrude Stein decreed: "Twentieth century literature is Gertrude Stein." The four big American writers were, according to Stein, Edgar Allen Poe, Walt Whitman, Henry James and herself.

Edward Titus published the memoirs of famous Montparnasse model Kiki with the English translation by Putnam. The introduction was written by Hemingway.

Cross Blvd. Raspail and walk down the other side.

35. Hôtel Carlton-Palace
207, blvd. Raspail

Because of the importance of European musicians Stravinsky, Ravel, Schönberg, Strauss and Satie, many young Americans studied music in Paris with Nadia Boulanger. This was considered the culmination of their professional education. Aaron Copland wrote, "In America, musical training was predominantly Germanic and old-fashioned. But, in Paris, Boulanger knew pre-Bach to post-Stravinsky . . . cold." Copland resided in the hotel in 1921-22.

Continue down the boulevard to Rue Campagne-Première and turn left at the corner.

36. Studio of Man Ray
31, rue Campagne-Première

For a year and a half, beginning July 1922, Man Ray lived in a small studio-darkroom. Into the room he crammed a bed, three large cameras and lights. A small closet served as the darkroom.

Kiki, who had been a Montparnasse model and mistress since she was fourteen years old, lived with Man Ray for six years. She was often his model, and also sat for Chaim Soutine, Maurice Utrillo, Marc Chagall and Amedeo Modigliani.

Since Man Ray photographed Gertrude Stein so often over many years, he claimed to be her official photographer. Stein wrote that she was fascinated with the way he used lights and always came home from her sittings pleased.

37. Hôtel Istria, Residence of Man Ray and Erik Satie 29, rue Campagne-Première

In 1931, Man Ray moved to this hotel from the studio at Number 31.

He had separated from Kiki and was making enough money to afford a professional studio.

French writer Maurice Sachs called Man Ray "one of the most talented and best-loved Parisian photographers." It was his photographs of the Paris *beau monde* (beautiful people) that made him wealthy, but he also produced art portraits of all the major figures of literature, such as Joyce, Pound, and Hemingway.

This was also where the composer Erik Satie lived out his last bleak years of self-inflicted poverty. He once wrote, "Before writing a work, I walk around it several times, accompanied by myself." Like the surrealists, Satie saw the necessity of shocking the public. In 1916, he collaborated with Jean Cocteau on the historic *Parade* for Diaghilev's Ballets Russes. The work expresses the whole artistic attitude of French art in the twenties humorously mixed with a combination of jazz and popular French dance music in an absurdist spirit. The sets and costumes were designed by Picasso and combined his harlequin and geometric-cubist periods. In the program notes, Apollinaire used the word "surrealism" to describe the piece. The performance received scathing reviews from the conservative critics.

While working together, Picasso invited Satie to meet Gertrude Stein. She remembered him as a charming dinner guest. Through a long friendship with Virgil Thomson, Stein developed an appreciation of Satie's music.

Satie was as eccentric as he was unpretentious, modestly shunning the limelight that should have been shown on so innovative an artist. He never bathed in water, preferring to rub himself down thoroughly with pumice stone once a month. When he moved here, he was in constant pain from cirrhosis of the liver and pleurisy. From here he was moved to St. Joseph's hospital in Paris, where he died at fifty-nine in July 1925. After his death, many years' worth of correspondences to him from some of most important artists, philosophers, and composers and writers of the twentieth century were found under the bed, all unopened and apparently unread.

Igor Stravinsky, who first met Satie at Claude Debussy's house, said, "I liked him right away. He was a crafty fox, full

Man Ray.
Photo credit: Gisèle Freund, courtesy of Photo Researchers.

of slyness and intelligently naughty." To the end Satie could not lose his sense of play.

38. Studio of Malvina Hoffman
17, rue Campagne-Première

Walking through this charming and picturesque impasse will delight anyone who enters. Somewhere in this quaint spot, possibly in the three-story building on your left with the bas-relief above the door, is the location of Malvina Hoffman's studio. Could the sculpture have been done by Hoffman? But then the old charming building on the other side also resembles a studio. Hoffman lived on the third floor of one of the buildings. Robert Bacon, the American Ambassador to France, was the subject of her first commissioned work in 1910. When Helena Rubenstein had the headquarters of her cosmetics empire built on New York's fashionable Fifth Avenue, she hired Hoffman to sculpt bas-reliefs.

39. Residence of Matthew Josephson and Arthur and Florence Gilliam Moss
7, rue Campagne-Première

Dada biographer Matthew Josephson, in 1921, was struggling to survive in a cheap, poorly furnished studio here. He joined fellow Dadaists Tristan Tzara and Man Ray in long evenings with the Rue Blomet Group. Josephson is probably best known for his biographies of Victor Hugo, Emile Zola, Stendhal and Thomas Edison.

Arthur Moss and Florence Gilliam Moss, publishers of *Gargoyle* also lived here. With the journal's demise in 1922—it survived for one year—Gilliam became the Paris correspondent for *Theater Magazine* and *Theater Arts* and wrote reviews for the Paris *Tribune*. Like other true expatriate women (Beach, Barney, Stein and Toklas), she never anticipated leaving France, but, in 1941, she withdrew to New York.

Turn right at Blvd. du Montparnasse and cross the broad street after about two blocks.

40. La Closerie des Lilas
171, blvd. du Montparnasse

"I went . . . up the Notre-Dame-des-Champs to the Closerie des Lilas. I sat in a corner with the afternoon light coming in over my shoulder and wrote in the notebook. The waiter brought me a café crème and I drank half of it when it cooled and left it on the table while I wrote."

Ernest Hemingway. Photo by Sylvia Beach at Shakespeare and Company. Courtesy of the Princeton University Library, Sylvia Beach Collection.

In *A Moveable Feast*, Hemingway tells of composing a majority of *The Sun Also Rises* and looking out on the statue of one of his favorite military heroes, Marshal Ney. In good weather, Hemingway and his frequent companion, John Dos Passos, sat at a table placed on the triangle of garden between the pavement of the two boulevards. At other times, beneath an actual lilac plant blooming in the Closerie, they read to each other from their favorite book, the New Testament.

While seated with F. Scott Fitzgerald one day, Hemingway was asked by Fitzgerald to read the manuscript of *The Great Gatsby*. After reading it, he wrote, "If he could write a book as fine as *The Great Gatsby*, I was sure he could write an even better one."

Look for the brass plates that mark the favorite seats of famous patrons André Gide, Amedeo Modigliani and Guillaume Apollinaire. Vladimir Lenin and Leon Trotsky would take the table near the entrance to the bar for a few games of chess.

WALK FIVE

THE HEART OF BOHEMIA

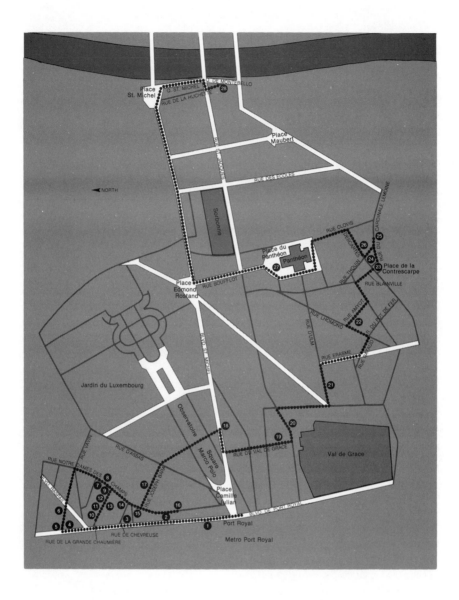

WALK V

Métro: Port Royal; Buses: 21 & 68

Exit the Métro on Blvd. du Montparnasse at Port Royal, turn right, and walk west on Montparnasse. The first landmark is across the street.

1. Residence of Katherine Anne Porter
166, blvd. du Montparnasse

Described as a "writer's writer," Katherine Anne Porter relates her first venture to Europe, by ship from Mexico to Germany, in *Ship of Fools*. The character Mary Treadwell reveals Porter's memories of Paris:

> *"I want to live in that dark alley named Impasse Deux-Anges (St-Germain-des-Prés) and have those little pointed jeweled blue velvet shoes at the Cluny copied and get my perfumes from Malinard's and go to Schiaparelli's Spring Show . . . I'll never leave Paris again . . . if every soul left it one day and grass grew in the pavements, I'd want to live there."*

Continue along Blvd. du Montparnasse.

2. Formerly Hôtel Venetia
159, blvd. du Montparnasse

Edna St. Vincent Millay was in Paris for sixteen months before her mother joined her. Millay had been so lonely in April and May of 1922 that she invited her mother to come. *Vanity Fair,* in the November 1922 issue, published Millay's article, "Diary of an American Art Student in Paris Showing How She Succeeded in Going to the Louvre Every Day."

3. Le Jockey
127, blvd. du Montparnasse

The Jockey was opened in 1922 by painter Hilaire Hiler. On the walls, Hiler painted bistro and cabaret scenes. Later, he changed his artistic style to exact and mathematical works, then became an abstract expressionist.

Almost everyone who was anybody in the modern literary, art and music scene in Paris appeared at tables here. Regular habitués were Jean Cocteau, Man Ray, Robert McAlmon, Marcel Duchamp and Louis Aragon.

Still on Blvd. du Montparnasse, cross Blvd. Raspail.

4. Café de la Rotonde
103, blvd. du Montparnasse

"You can find anything you're looking for at the Rotonde except serious artists. The trouble is that people who go on a tour of the Latin Quarter look in the Rotonde and think they are seeing an assembly of the real artists of Paris,"
wrote Hemingway.

Home of the revolutionaries and bohemians, the Rotonde consisted of a café, grill room, nightclub and artist's gallery. Guillaume Apollinaire, Pablo Picasso, Max Jacob and Amedeo Modigliani were often here. When Edna St. Vincent Millay's mother stayed with her, they ate here every day. In a letter to her sister, Millay referred to the café as "the famous sink of corruption of the Latin Quarter."

5. Café Le Sélect
99, blvd. du Montparnasse

Each café, popular with artists and writers, was uniquely ambiant. Le Sélect hummed with talk of horses and racing. After Harold Stearns returned to New York, he wrote that Le Sélect was a "seething madhouse of drunks, semi-drunks, quarter-drunks and sober maniacs. It was a useless silly life and I have missed every day of it since."

One could meet everyone here. Hemingway and Morley Callaghan usually sat at the first table to the right of the door that goes into the main bar.

One evening, as Callaghan was on his way to meet his wife at Le Sélect, he met Hemingway and Joan Miró. Hemingway suggested that they walk along with Callaghan. When the three arrived at the café, Hemingway introduced Loretta Callaghan to Miró and they remained for the evening at the table. Callaghan later remarked that Miró had sensed that Loretta Callaghan wanted to meet him, and had gone out of his way to please her.

Turn the corner to your right onto Rue Vavin.

6. Residence of Harold Stearns
50, rue Vavin

Arriving in 1921, Stearns was the Paris correspondent for the Baltimore *Sun* by 1930 and wrote a daily column on horse racing for the *Chicago Tribune*. In Hemingway's novel, *The Sun Also Rises*, Stearns is portrayed as Harvey Stone. Unable to support

La Rotonde.
Photo credit: Mary Ellen Jordan Haight.

Aux Deux Magots.
Photo credit: Mary Ellen Jordan Haight.

his heavy drinking, but able to support the nearby cafés and bars, he returned to America broke in 1934, and *Rediscovering America* was published within a year of his return. Stearns had advised young Americans to live abroad to increase their creativity; yet, he did his best writing in in his home country.

Continue up Rue Vavin, crossing Blvd. Raspail, and turn right at Rue Notre-Dame-des-Champs.

7. Residence of Ezra and Dorothy Pound
70 bis, rue Notre-Dame-des-Champs

The pavillon standing in the courtyard was home to Ezra Pound and his wife Dorothy (*née* Shakespear) in 1921. Their apartment on the second floor in the rear overlooked a garden. The residence was described by Hemingway as being "as poor as Gertrude Stein's was rich." The low tea table was constructed from rough boards by Pound, who also built two large armchairs from boards and canvases. Packing cases served as tables and other furniture. According to Hemingway,

"It had very good light and was heated by a stove and it had paintings by Japanese artists that Ezra knew . . . . Dorothy's paintings I liked very much and I thought Dorothy was very beautiful and built wonderfully."

Although the furnishings were poor, Pound's parties were lavish. Widely known for these extraordinary affairs at which he often danced wildly, Pound was a superb host.

"Whoever has not seen Ezra Pound kicking up fantastic heels in a highly personal Charleston, closing his eyes as his toes nimbly scattered right and left, has missed one of the spectaculars which reconcile us to life," commented Sisley Huddleston.

Pound arrived in Paris in 1920 to "save American letters from premature suicide and decomposition." After living in London for fourteen years, he was now considered a major poet. While living at this address, he worked on the *Cantos.* He also wrote an opera, *Testament,* selections from which were successfully performed in Paris in 1925.

After hearing from Brancusi that Pound's latest opera, *Villon,* had been performed at the Théâtre des Champs-Elysees and that Brancusi pronounced it a scandal, William Carlos Williams remarked, "Pound writing an opera? Why he doesn't know one note from another."

The Pounds permanently moved to Italy and from 1934 to 1936, Katherine Anne Porter, already a prominent author, occupied the pavilion. As a result of her successful book of short stories, *Flowering Judas,* Porter lived in Paris for four years on a Guggenheim fellowship.

Sylvia Beach recalled visiting Porter and her enormous cat and eating in the pleasant courtyard. At Shakespeare and Company, Beach introduced Hemingway to Katherine Anne Porter with the comment, "I want the two best modern American writers to know each other." When Porter married Eugene Pressly in March 1933, Beach and Adrienne Monnier signed the marriage certificate. In the fall of 1936, Porter returned to her native Texas, but she remained a lifelong friend of Beach.

According to Porter, "the twenties in Paris were shallow and silly." She did not consider F. Scott Fitzgerald a great writer and didn't think much of Ernest Hemingway either. "I consider Hemingway a fraud and not eligible for any serious comment."

8. Residence of Alice B. Toklas and Harriet Levy
75, rue Notre-Dame-des-Champs

Alice B. Toklas sailed for France in September 1907, accompanied by her friend from San Francisco, Harriet Levy. After staying at a couple of hotels, the pair rented a four-room-plus-kitchen apartment on the first floor. The sunny space did not include a bathroom. Levy provided rugs and a Renaissance table. Toklas hemstitched the mesh curtains and purchased camel-back cushions.

In the mornings, Toklas would walk the short distance across Montparnasse to the Stein home on Rue de Fleurus, where she typed Gertrude Stein's previous night's work. One night, while returning via Rue de Rennes, she was frightened by footsteps following her. It was Henri Rousseau, who gently scolded her for being out alone after dark. He walked her home while elaborating upon her resemblance to his dead wife.

Levy returned to San Francisco in 1912 and Toklas moved to Rue de Fleurus with Gertrude and Leo Stein. When Leo Stein moved to Italy two years later, Gertrude Stein and Alice B. Toklas began the household partnership that spanned thirty-two years.

9. Studio of Malvina Hoffman
72, rue Notre-Dame-des-Champs

Standing across the street from the three-story building and looking closely at the roof, you can see the skylights that provided north light to the studio of sculptor Malvina Hoffman. She wrote that the studio was a stage setting worthy of a scene in *La Boheme*. Hoffman arrived in Paris in 1910 at the age of twenty-three to study sculpture. In 1927, she purchased a lot in Paris and designed the house she was to occupy in outer Montparnasse the next summer. She worked there until 1938, when she left to spend the war years in America, then returned in 1948. When she finally sold the house in 1961, she had been associated with Paris for almost fifty years.

At the corner, turn right onto Rue de la Grande Chaumière.

10. Hôtel Liberia
9, rue de la Grande-Chaumière

Author Nathanael West stayed here for twelve weeks in 1926. Like many writers in the twenties, he came to Paris to escape what he considered the oppressive cultural climate in the United States. His 1933 novel, *Miss Lonelyhearts,* reflects this escapism.

From 1935 until his death in 1940, West was a Hollywood screenwriter and authored *The Day of the Locust* (1939), one of the best of the Hollywood novels. West was killed in an automobile accident on December 22, 1944 in southern California, the day after fellow author and neighbor F. Scott Fitzgerald had died of a heart attack. West's new bride, Eileen McKenney, whose antics inspired her sister's play, *My Sister Eileen,* was also killed in the senseless accident.

11. Académie de la Grande-Chaumière
14, rue de la Grande-Chaumière

Many Americans studied art at this academy, preferring the school to the Art Students League in New York because of the more serious attitude of the students here. Alexander Calder arrived in France in 1926 to learn painting and recorded, "I went to the Grande-Chaumière to draw. Here there were no teachers, just a nude model and everyone was drawing by himself."

12. Studio of Janet Scudder
Rue de la Grande-Chaumière

Somewhere on this short street in 1922 was the studio of Janet Scudder. A sculptor specializing in garden statuary such as fauns and boys on dolphins, each Saturday Scudder held "afternoons," which were attended by her friend from the pre-war days,

Gertrude Stein. Commented Stein, "There are only two perfectly solemn things on earth, the doughboys and Janet Scudder." Consequently Scudder was nicknamed "Doughboy" because she had "all the subtlety of the doughboy and all his nice ways and all his lonesomeness."

13. Residence of Amedeo Modigliani
Rue de la Grand-Chaumière

Somewhere on this block, Amedeo Modigliani lived in a building owned by Nancy Cunard. Model Jeanne Héburterne, the subject of many of his paintings and the mother of his child, shared the simple room from 1919 until the death of Modigliani in 1926 at thirty-six years of age.

Modigliani would spread his canvases against trees, walls of houses and on benches. With his dark, curly hair and dressed in corduroy pants and knitted jersey tops, he looked like a French working man. Modigliani left a wealth of portraits of members of Paris bohemia, including one of Jean Cocteau. He also painted some of the most celebrated nudes in modern art. Before his early death from tubular meningitis and malnutrition, Modigliani declared, "Jeanne and I, we've agreed on an eternal joy." Pregnant with their second child, Héburterne committed suicide the day after his death.

Returning once again to Rue Notre-Dame-des-Champs, turn right. Continue for one block until you reach little Rue de Chevreuse on the right.

14. Reid Hall
4, rue de Chevreuse

Reid Hall was established in 1922 as a center for university women of the United States and other nations of the world through the generosity of Elizabeth Mills Reid, wife of the American Ambassador to France. It now houses the women students of nine American universities. In 1894, when it was the American University Women's Paris Club, sculptor Janet Scudder stayed here.

"The students in the house represented every branch of art— painting, sculpture, music and architecture. Just the mere fact of living there surrounded by so many of them, all working with enthusiasm, was tremendously stimulating."

André Breton.
Photo credit: Gisèle Freund, courtesy of Photo Researchers.

Samuel Beckett.
Photo credit: Gisèle Freund, courtesy of Photo Researchers.

The fountains and garden figures sculpted by Scudder are displayed now in the Metropolitan Museum in New York and in many private gardens.

It is all right to step inside the flagstone courtyard and visit the large garden behind it.

Return to the corner of Chevreuse and continue down Notre-Dame-des-Champs.

15. Residence of James McNeil Whistler
86, rue Notre-Dame-des-Champs

James McNeil Whistler lived in this tired-looking building from 1892 to 1902. He died a year later. The narrow, twisting stairway leading to his top floor studio, which had a view of the Jardin du Luxumbourg, can still be seen through the glass front. Here he worked on his etchings, producing around four hundred plates. Whistler also wrote essays, one of which is *The Gentle Art of Making Enemies.* He was recognized as a man of sincere impulses in human relations, and was also witty, gentle, audacious and genuinely kind.

Famous in America for the portrait of his mother which hangs in the Musée d'Orsay, Whistler was an outspoken defender of the value of modern art. He once testified in court on behalf of impressionist painting, insisting that although some modern paintings could be turned upside-down or sideways without changing the desired effect, they were nonetheless works of art. About the portrait of his mother he once wrote, "For me, it is interesting because it is a portrait of my mother, but the public cannot and should not be concerned with the model's identity. A painting should stand purely on the merit of its composition."

16. Residence of Ernest and Hadley Hemingway
113, rue Notre-Dame-des-Champs

The old cobblestone courtyard is all that remains of the sawmill over which Ernest and Hadley Hemingway and their young son lived in 1924. The small square with three trees is still visible, enclosed by old houses on your right that look as if they were here in the twenties. At the top of the wooden stairs on the second story of the old building that stood here, the Hemingways lived in a medium-sized living room, a small dining room, one little bedroom with a stove for heat, and a dressing room where John Hadley (Bumby) slept. There was a tiny kitchen and a toilet where the linens and bath supplies were kept. It was to this home that Hemingway carried the large bright canvas, *The Farm,* painted by Joan Miró. With financial help from friends, he paid five thousand francs for it as a thirty-fourth birthday gift to his wife. After their divorce, Hemingway borrowed the painting in the thirties and never returned it.

In *A Moveable Feast,* Hemingway writes of walking home from the Closerie des Lilas to the flat over the sawmill and his "waiting wife," son, and cat, F. Puss. He once said to her about Gertrude Stein, whom he had just left, "You know, Gertrude is nice, anyway." Hadley answered, "Of course, Tatie." "But she does talk a lot of rot sometimes," answered Hemingway. "I never hear her," she said. "I'm a wife. It's her friend that talks to me."

During this period, after the Hemingways had returned from Canada, he decided to devote all his time to writing fiction. The first draft of *The Sun Also Rises* was composed here in just six weeks.

Walk back two blocks, then turn right onto Rue Joseph Bara.

17. Studio of Moïse Kisling
Rue Joseph Bara

When painter Marc Chagall was forced to flee his native Russia after the revolution, he returned to Paris in 1923 and to the company of his fellow Eastern European refugees. In the new Russia, Chagall's modern paintings had come into conflict with collectivist attitudes towards art.

Chagall was frequently seen in the studio of Russian painter Moïse Kisling, which was located somewhere on this short street. Because of his warm personality, Kisling welcomed the painters, dealers and models of Montparnasse to his room here and it became the center of the neighborhood social life. The young model, Kiki, often posed for him; it was Kisling's translucently veiled nude portraits of her that made him famous.

Continue across Rue d'Assas onto Rue Michelet and through Observatoire to Blvd. St.-Michel. The next landmark is across the street.

18. Hôtel des Mines
125, blvd. St-Michel

Lithuanian sculptor Jacques Lipchitz came to Paris in 1908 to study at the Ecole des Beaux-Arts. When he met Gertrude Stein in 1915, he was involved in cubism with his friends Picasso, Gris and Modigliani. Although Stein's interest was also in cubism, she was interested in collecting paintings, not sculpture. When, in 1920, she agreed to sit for a portrait-bust, it was partly because she found Lipchitz charming and an "excellent gossip." At one sitting, she asked the question "Who, besides Shakespeare and myself, do you think there is in English literature?" His answer is not recorded.

The bust depicts Stein as a sleek buddha, with a top knot and the eyes hollowed out because he had trouble achieving the "shadowed introspection" he felt characterized her eyes.

Immediately before Hitler's occupation of Paris in 1940, Lipchitz fled to the south of France, then to America. In 1962, he returned to Europe, but to Italy rather than France, where he worked prodigiously until his death ten years later.

Turn right and walk one block, then left onto Rue du Val-de-Grâce.

19. Studio of Man Ray
8, rue du Val-de-Grâce

American surrealist painter turned photographer, Man Ray, had become such a success by 1929 that he could afford two studios. He not only photographed many of the art circle of Montparnasse, but also the wealthy Parisians. His unique studies include mobiles of clothespins and clothes hampers, an egg framed by a toilet seat, a jar filled with ball bearings in oil and the dismantled insides of an alarm clock in a case filled with tobacco smoke. It was in 1929 that he did his self-portrait with an alarm clock, pistol in his hand and his head in a hangman's noose.

With Val-de-Grâce, the military hospital, in front, continue to Place Lavarin, turn left up Rue St.-Jacques and cross to the other side of the street.

20. Schola Cantorum
269, rue St.-Jacques

The Schola Cantorum was founded in 1896 as a monument to Cesar Franck, and emphasized formal training in music, dance and drama. In 1919, after service with the American forces in France in World War I composer Cole Porter studied here.

Born in 1866, Erik Satie had played piano in Montmartre cafés as a teenager. In full bohemian attire—velvet coat, flowing tie, soft felt hat, beard and monocle, he was infamously eccentric and looked upon as a serious composer. At eighteen years old he began the composition of his most famous songs for piano, the three *Gymnopedies,* which he completed in 1889.

In the same year Satie dropped out of the wild activity of cabaret life, moved to a Parisian suburb and then lived many years in silence and hibernation. Sixteen years later, at forty years of age, Erik Satie applied for a scholarship to attend the music school. A draft of a letter to the director of the Schola Cantorum requesting scholarship help stated,

"I am a poor artist up against the difficulties of life; there it is absolutely impossible for me to pay the tuition price required of students taking his course."

He apparently received the tuition because, in 1908, he received a diploma "to devote himself exclusively to the study of composition."

Satie's elegant refusal to write traditionally elaborate symphonic pieces, and his disinterest in producing the full orchestral sounds of previous composers gave him a reputation for composing piano pieces that were simple but profound. Satie's innovative simplicity influenced many composers and prefaced the experimental dissonance of the twentieth-century modern composers.

Continue up St.-Jacques to the first corner, turn right, then left on Rue d'Ulm.

21. Ecole Normale Supérieure Rue d'Ulm

Passing the residence halls of the prestigious school where many great women and men of letters studied, one might have heard Samuel Beckett, in the late evening hours, playing sad Irish songs on his flute to the entertainment of the students. Teaching only one student allowed him to sleep until noon. A little while later he and the student would read Shakespeare in the Dôme. He stayed up late in the evening working on the play *Waiting for Godot,* set in the neighborhood, in which he describes the local scene and its residents.

In 1928, the twenty-two-year-old Beckett, a recent graduate of Trinity College in Dublin, arrived in Paris to take a two-year appointment as lecturer in English. The tall, thin young Irishman with thick glasses had read James Joyce's *Ulysses* and gratefully worked without pay reading to Joyce, running errands for him and doing research, demonstrating his admiration for his fellow Irish author. In 1930, he returned to Trinity as a teacher of French, but came back to Paris in 1938 to make his permanent home. He was now so poor he could not afford a library card at Shakespeare and Company. Instead he would read the books in the store. Since 1945, he has been writing in French. The Nobel Prize of Literature was awarded him in 1969. A recluse, Beckett is now in his eighties and still writing vigorously. Recently asked if he and his wife had ever had children, Beckett replied that he didn't know whether they had or not.

Follow Rue d'Ulm, then right onto Rue Erasme. After one block, bear left onto Rue Rataud, and again left at the next corner on Rue Lhomond, and right on Rue Amyot.

22. Residence of Jeanne Héburterne's Family 5, rue Amyot

From her family's apartment on this small insignificant street, Jeanne Héburterne threw herself from the fifth floor balcony to her death on the cobblestones below. Depressed over the loss of her lover, Amedeo Modigliani, she committed suicide the day after his death. The lovers are buried together at Père Lachaise cemetery.

Continue to the next corner and turn left, then right onto the short Rue Blainville to its end.

23. Place de la Contrescarpe

The characters Vladimir and Estragon in Beckett's *Waiting for Godot* were pictured here, leaning against a tree, sharing a bottle of wine. The picturesque area is mainly inhabited by *clochards,* or hobos, who can be seen in the winter huddled over heating ducts and in the summer lounging against the center trees, existing on spoils from the neighboring markets and change from the tourists and shoppers of the adjacent narrow, crowded market street, Rue Mouffetard.

In two of his books, Hemingway describes Place de la Contrescarpe:

". . . the flower sellers dyed their flowers in the street, and the dye ran over the paving . . . and the old men and women,

always drunk on bad wine, and the children with their noses
running in the cold, the smell of dirty sweat and poverty and
drunkenness at the Café des Amateurs . . . the cesspool of the
place.'' (The Snows of Kilimanjaro)

In *A Moveable Feast,* Hemingway writes of rainy winter
weather when the cold wind would strip the leaves from the
trees.

Walk east across the square to Rue de Cardinal-Lemoine.

24. Residence of Ernest and Hadley Hemingway 74, rue du Cardinal-Lemoine

Up five flights of narrow winding stairs, through a door under
the roof, is the first Paris home the Hemingways shared in
1922. All the rooms had sharp and obtuse angles and unexpected
planes. The bedroom contained a large gilt-trimmed imitation
mahogany bed and a coal burning fireplace furnished the only
heat. The dining room—there was no living room—was crowded
with an ugly oak table and chairs. Only one person at a time could
squeeze into the small kitchen with its two burner gas stove.
Hemingway described the apartment as having pictures they
liked, a fine view—"a cheerful gay flat." For the struggling writer
and his wife, lunch was an egg, boiled potatoes and wine. After
Gertrude Stein met them, she shared the spartan lunch and read
his short story, "Up In Michigan." According to Hemingway, her
opinion of it was:

"It's good . . . That's not the question at all. But it is inaccroch-
able. That means it is like a picture that a painter paints and
then he cannot hang it when he has a show and nobody will
buy it because they cannot hang it either.''

An evening out for the Hemingways was often spent next
door at the bal musette, now a discotéque. The dance hall was
dark and narrow with wooden tables and benches along the walls.
The small space for dancing was occupied by couples who purchased tokens in advance for a dance. Everyone could dance with
everyone else. Although Hadley Hemingway was said to be occasionally frightened by the rough men who asked her to dance,
Ernest Hemingway seemed to revel in the smoky atmosphere.

When Ezra Pound's infamous parties became too riotous for
his Rue Notre-Dame-des-Champs pavilion, he invited the merry
makers to the bal. After a while the revelers were too raucous for
even the dance hall and Pound discontinued the weekly soirées.

Proceed down the hill and at the next landmark walk through the narrow alley to the houses at the rear.

25. Residence of James Joyce
71, rue du Cardinal-Lemoine

James Joyce completed his monumental and controversial work, *Ulysses,* here in a flat borrowed from French writer Valéry Larbaud. Leaving his home to live in the country during 1921 and 1922, Larbaud believed Joyce would be more comfortable here than in a hotel. Said Larbaud of Joyce, "My admiration for Joyce is such that I am sure he is, of all contemporaries, the only one who will pass into posterity." Larbaud was one of a group of young French writers published by Adrienne Monnier in the *Gazette des Amis des Livres.*

Joyce was very concerned about the opinions and response to his works by French writers and critics. The writers of Larbaud's generation were favorable to Joyce, but Paul Valéry, Paul Claudel, Marcel Proust and André Gide, born about ten years earlier, were either very critical of or indifferent to Joyce.

In *Paris Was Our Mistress,* Samuel Putnam describes an evening when Gertrude Stein was asked about Joyce:

"Joyce, she admitted, is good. (the italics were in her voice.) He is a good writer. People like him because he is incomprehensible and anybody can understand him. But who came first, Gertrude Stein or James Joyce? Do not forget that my first great book, Three Lives, was published in 1908. That was long before Ulysses. But Joyce has done something. His influence, however, is local."

Backtrack to Rue Thouin. Walk one short block to Rue Descartes and go right.

26. Studio of Ernest Hemingway
39, rue Descartes

In 1922, in a top floor room where French writer Paul Verlaine had spent his final years in poor health, Ernest Hemingway would lie on a bed composing his earliest stories. To have a quiet place to work, he paid sixty francs a month. On cold days, he roasted chestnuts in the small fireplace. When the room was too cold, the nearby cafés provided a warm environment in which to work. The glass-enclosed terraces were heated by charcoal braziers. As he sat nursing the one café crème he could afford, he composed in blue French school notebooks. The pages were later typed on a Corona portable typewriter given him by his wife for Christmas.

At the age of twenty-one, in October 1917, John Dos Passos came to France to live here in what he described as "a small chilly room." The rent was only eight francs a week. Planning to study architecture, Dos Passos painted and then wrote. He soon volunteered as a driver in the American Ambulance Field Service, described by Malcolm Cowley as "a college extension course for a generation of writers."

Continue up Rue Descartes and turn left at the first corner, passing the Lycée Henri IV, one of Paris' most prestigious high schools, attended by such notables as Alfred Jarry. It is also where Jean-Paul Sartre taught. Go left at the Panthéon toward Rue Soufflot.

27. Place du Panthéon

Rodin's famous sculpture, *The Thinker,* was originally placed in front of the Panthéon. After his death the French government moved it to the Hôtel Biron, site of the Musée Rodin. Emile-Antoine Bourdelle, student of Rodin, said of his mentor, "Rodin put the breath of life in the stone. He made his men and women truly human and in that he stands alone."

Dada and surrealist writer André Breton lived in the nearby Hôtel des Grands Hommes. The dada movement, precursor of surrealism, pushed the concept of individualism to the extreme: there were no laws which man must obey. Nothing would be real or true except the individual pursuing his individual whims. The philosophy produced bizarre plays. Tristan Tzara, who with Frances Picabia founded dada, was born in Rumania in 1896. Dada, a nursery name for rocking horse, reflects the meaninglessness of a culture's symbols. In Zurich in 1916, Tzara delivered the first dada manifesto at the Café Terasse, accompanied by Hans Arp, who had a brioche hanging from his left nostril. When he arrived in Paris in 1920, Tzara was escorted by Picabia to Rue Blomet, where he was excitedly questioned by Miró, Masson, Artaud, and Soupault, who had eagerly awaited his pronouncements.

Picabia eventually introduced Tzara to Gertrude Stein, who was unimpressed by his proclamations. Thereupon Tzara declared, "The true dadaists are against dada."

Once during an argument with Gertrude Stein over the worth of his surrealist poetry, Pablo Picasso said defensively, "My poetry is good. Breton says so."

"Breton admires anything to which he can sign his name," retorted Stein.

Hemingway wrote about walking down Rue Descartes in the cold rain of winter.

> *"I walked down past the Lycée Henri Quatre and the ancient church of St.-Etienne-du Mont and the windswept Place du Panthéon and cut in for shelter to the right and finally came out on the lee side of the Boulevard St.-Michel and walked on down it past the Cluny and the Boulevard St.-Germain until I came to a good café that I knew on the Place St.-Michel."*

There he orders a rum St.-James.

Proceed east along Quai. St.-Michel. Continue to Quai de Montebello. Walk V ends on the Quai de Montebello in the shadow of Notre Dame Cathedral.

28. Shakespeare and Company
37, rue de la Bûcherie

In early June of 1940, Rue de l'Odéon outside the original Shakespeare and Company streamed with people evacuating Paris. Some headed for the railway stations, while others carried their belongings on their backs or pushed loaded wheelbarrows, as they fled by bicycle or on foot.

When the bombings began, Sylvia Beach was determined to keep the bookstore open and resisted all warnings from the American embassy to leave Paris. Virgil Thomson made his way to the Pyrenees, then to America by way of Lisbon, Portugal, a route also taken by Man Ray, Salvador Dali and Robert McAlmon. Gisèle Freund sailed for Argentina, Josephine Baker reached her chateau in the South, Jules Romains and André Breton resettled in America and Gertrude Stein and Alice B. Toklas were protected by public officials in eastern France.

Gertrude Stein predicted the war would be over when she had cut all the box hedges in the gardens at Billignin. On the eighth of August, she completed the cutting. With the war not over, she wrote in *A Picture of Occupied France:*

> *". . . perhaps everybody will find out, as the French know so well, that the winner loses, and everybody will be, too, like*

the French, that is, tremendously occupied with the business of daily living, and that will be enough.''

The final three days of free Paris were described by Beach:
''. . . a lovely June day in 1940. Sunny with blue skies. Only about 25,000 people were left in Paris . . . through our tears [we] watched the refugees moving through the city.''

For the rest of 1940, Shakespeare and Company stayed open with just fifty-three library members, including Simone de Beauvoir. When an angry German officer threatened to confiscate the books in the store after America had entered the war in 1941, Beach closed Shakespeare and Company forever.

"There is never any ending to Paris," wrote Ernest Hemingway,
"and the memory of each person who has lived in it differs from that of any other. We always returned to it no matter who we were or how it was changed or with what difficulties, or ease, it could be reached. Paris was always worth it and you received return for whatever you brought to it. But this is how Paris was in the early days when we were very poor and very happy."

''. . . The twentieth century,'' wrote Gertrude Stein,
"is a century which sees the earth as no one has ever seen it, the earth has a splendor that it never has had, and as everything destroys itself in the twentieth century and nothing continues, so then the twentieth century has a splendor which is its own and Picasso is of this century, he has the strange quality of an earth that one has never seen and of things destroyed as they have never been destroyed.''

BIBLIOGRAPHY

Aldridge, John W.. *After the Last Generation.* New York: McGraw Hill, Inc., 1951.

Allan, Tony. *The Glamour Years Paris 1919-1940.* New York: Gallery Books, W.H. Smith Publishers, Inc., 1977.

Anderson, Chester C.. *James Joyce and His World.* London: Peter Owen, 1966.

Anderson, Margaret. *My Thirty Years' War: An Autobiography by Margeret Anderson.* New York: Covice, Friede, 1930.

Anderson, Sherwood and Gertrude Stein. *Sherwood Anderson/Gertrude Stein Correspondence and Personal Essays.* Ray Lewis White, ed., Chapel Hill, NC: University of North Carolina Press, 1972.

Baker, Carlos. *Ernest Hemingway: A Life Story.* New York: Charles Scribner's Sons, 1969.

Barnes, Djuna. *Nightwood.* New York: New Directions Publishing Corp., 1982.

Beach, Sylvia. *Shakespeare & Company.* New York: Harcourt, Brace, 1959.

Bell, Millicent. *Edith Wharton & Henry James.* New York: George Braziller, Inc., 1965.

Benstock, Shari. *Women of the Left Bank, Paris, 1900-1940.* Austin, TX: University of Texas Press, 1986.

Berg, A. Scott. *Max Perkins, Editor of Genius.* New York: Simon & Schuster, 1978.

Bergum, Edwin Berry. "Ernest Hemingway and the Psychology of the Lost Generation." In *The Novel and the World's Dilemma.* Oxford: Oxford University Press, 1947.

Bertrand, Jules. *Paris 1870-1945.* London: 1946.

Brinnen, John Malcolm. *The Third Rose: Gertrude Stein and Her World.* Boston: Little, Brown & Co., 1959.

Bruccoli, Matthew J. and Duggan, Margaret M.. *Correspondence of F. Scott Fitzgerald.* New York: Random House, 1980.

Burnett, Avis. *Gertrude Stein.* New York: Atheneum, 1972.

Callaghan, Morley. *That Summer in Paris.* New York: Coward- McCann, 1963.

Charles-Roux, Edmonde. *Chanel and Her World.* London: Vendome Press, 1979.

Chaters, James. *This Must Be the Place.* New York: Lee Furman, 1937.

Conrad, Barnaby III. "Museum of the Twentieth Century." In San Francisco *Chronicle Review,* (Dec. 1987): 15.

Cowley, Malcolm. *Exile's Return: A Literary Odyssey of the 1920s.* New York: Viking Press, 1951.

Cowley, Malcolm (ed.). *Writers at Work, The Paris Review Interviews, Second Series.* New York: Viking Press, 1963.

Cowley, Malcolm. *A Second Flowering: Works and Days,*

of the Lost Generation. New York: Viking Press, 1973.

Culbertson, Judi and Randall, Tom. *Permanent Parisians.* Chelsea: Chelsea Green Publishing Company, 1986.

Cunard, Nancy. *Nancy Cunard: Brave Poet, Indomitable Rebel, 1896-1965.* Hugh Ford, ed., Philadelphia: Chilton Book Co., 1968.

Donnelly, Honoria Murphy, with Billings, Richard N. *Sara and Gerald.* New York: Rhinehart & Winston, 1984.

Dos Passos, John. *The Best Times.* New York: Rhinehart & Winston, 1984.

Drutman, Irving. *Janet Flanner's World.* New York & London: Harcourt, Brace, Janovich, 1979.

Earnest, Ernest. *Expatriates and Patriots: American Artists, Scholars and Writers in Europe.* Durham, North Carolina: Duke University Press, 1968.

Fabe, Maxene. *Beauty Millionaire, The Life of Helena Rubenstein.* New York: Thomas Crowell Co., 1972.

Fitch, Noel Riley. *Sylvia Beach and the Lost Generation.* London: W.W. Norton & Co., 1983.

Fitzgerald, F. Scott. *Tender is the Night.* New York: Charles Scribner's Sons, 1933.

Flanner, Janet. *An American in Paris.* London: Hamish Hamilton, 1940.

Flanner, Janet. *Paris Was Yesterday.* London: Angus & Robertson, 1973.

Ford, Hugh. *Published in Paris.* New York: MacMillan, 1975.

Ford, Hugh. *Four Lives in Paris.* San Francisco: North Point Press, 1987.

Freund, Gisèle. *Gisele Freund, Photographer.* New York: Harry N. Abrams Publishers, 1985.

Freund, Gisèle. *James Joyce in Paris: His Final Years.* New York: Harcourt, Brace & World, Inc., 1965.

Gajdusek, Robert E.. *Hemingway's Paris.* New York: Scribner's, 1978.

Gide, André. *The Journals of André Gide 1899-1939.* Vol. II translated by Justin O'Brien, New York: Alfred Knopf, 1948.

Hemingway, Ernest. *The Sun Also Rises.* New York: Charles Scribner's Sons, 1926.

Hemingway, Ernest. *A Moveable Feast.* New York: Charles Scribner's Sons, 1964.

Hemingway, Ernest. *Islands in the Stream.* New York: Charles Scribner's Sons, 1970.

Hemingway, Leicester. *My Brother, Ernest Hemingway.* Cleveland: World, 1962.

Hobhouse, Janet. *Everybody Who Was Anybody: A Biography of Gertrude Stein.* New York: G.P. Putnam & Sons, 1975.

Horton, Philip. *Hart Crane.* New York: Viking Press, 1957.

Hotchner, A. E.. *Papa Hemingway.* New York: W.W. Norton & Co., 1983.

Huddleston, Sisley. *Paris Salons, Cafés, Studios.* New York: Blue Ribbon, 1928.

Hunter, Sam. *Modern French Painting, 1855-1956.* New York: Dell Publishing Inc., 1960.

Josephson, Matthew. *Life Among the Surrealists.* New York: Holt, Rhinehart & Winston, 1962.

Kert, Bernice. *The Hemingway Women.* New York: W.W. Norton & Co., 1983.

Landes, Allison and Sonia. *Pariswalks,* New York: A New Republic Book, Holt, Rinehart & Winston, 1982.

Le Central Cultural Américain. *Les Anneés Vingt: Ecrivains Américains Paris et Leurs Amis, 1920-1930.* Paris Exposition, 1959.

Leng, Felicity. "Hemingway's Paris." In *Paris Magazine,* Paris: Autumn 1984.

Lemaitre, Georges. *From Cubism to Surrealism in French Literature.* Cambridge, MA: Harvard University Press, 1941.

Lewis, R.W.B.. *Edith Wharton: A Biography.* New York: Harper & Row Publishers, 1975.

McAlmon, Robert and Boyle, Kay. *Being Geniuses Together, 1920-1930.* San Francisco: North Point Press, 1984.

Mellow, James. *Charmed Circle.* New York: Avon Books, 1982.

Mercure de France. *"Sylvia Beach (1887-1962)".* Paris: Memorial Edition to Sylvia Beach, 349, (Aug-Sept., 1936).

Meyers, Jeffrey. *Hemingway: A Biography.* New York: Harper & Row, Inc., 1985.

Milford, Nancy. *Zelda.* New York: Harper & Row, 1970.

Miller, Henry. *My Life & Times.* New York: Gemini Smith, Inc., 1974.

Miller, Henry. *Quiet Days in Clichy.* New York: Grove Press, 1978.

Monnier, Adrienne. *The Very Rich Hours of Adrienne Monnier.* Richard McDougall, translator, New York: Charles Scribner's Sons, 1976.

Monnier, Adrienne. *Rue de l'Odéon.* Paris: Editions Albin Michel, 1960.

Morley, Sheridan. *Oscar Wilde.* New York: Holt, Rinehart & Winston, 1976.

Morton, Brian N.. *Americans in Paris.* Ann Arbor: The Olivia & Hill Press, 1984.

Museum of Modern Art. *Four Americans in Paris.* Introduction by Margaret Potter. Essays by Douglas Cooper, Lucile and Leon Katz. New York: Museum of Modern Art, 1970.

Neogoe, Peter(ed.). *Americans Abroad.* The Hague: The Service Press, 1932.

Nin, Anaïs. *The Diary of Anaïs Nin 1934-1939*. Stuhlman, Gunther, ed., London: Peter Owen, 1966.

Nowell, Elizabeth. *Thomas Wolfe*. New York: Doubleday & Co., 1960.

Orwell, George. *Down and Out in Paris and London*. New York: 1961.

Paul, Elliot. *The Last Time I Saw Paris*. New York: Random House Inc., 1942.

Perlès, Alfred. *My Friend, Henry Miller*. New York: Belmont Books, 1962.

Poli, Bernard J.. *Ford Madox Ford and the* Transatlantic Review. Syracuse, N.Y: Syracuse University Press, 1967.

Porter, Katherine Anne. *Ship of Fools*. London: Panther Books, Granada Publishing Co., 1985.

Putnam, Samuel. *Paris Was Our Mistress*. New York: Viking Press, 1947.

Richardson, Joanna. *Colette*. New York: Dell Publishing Co., Inc., 1985.

Rogers, W.G.. *When This You See, Remember Me: Gertrude Stein in Person*. New York: Rinehart, 1948.

Rood, Karen Lane. "American Writers in Paris, 1920-1939" In *Dictionary of Literary Biography*. Detroit: Gale Research Co., 1980.

Schorer, Mark. *Sinclair Lewis: An American Life*. New York: McGraw-Hill Book Company Inc., 1961.

Shattuck, Roger. *The Banquet Years*. New York: Vintage Books, 1968.

Simon, Linda. *The Biography of Alice B. Toklas*. New York: Avon Books, 1977.

Stein, Gertrude. *Matisse, Picasso and Gertrude Stein with Two Shorter Pieces*. Paris: Plain Edition, 1933.

Stein, Gertrude. *Picasso*. London: Batsford Ltd., 1938.

Stein, Gertrude. *Wars I Have Seen*. New York: Random House, 1945.

Stein, Gertrude. *Everybody's Autobiography*. New York: Something Else Press, 1966.

Stein, Gertrude. *Selected Writings of Gertrude Stein*. Carl Van Vechten, ed. New York: Random House, 1946.

Stein, Gertrude. "Gertrude Stein: Letters to a Friend." Philip Galones(ed.). In *Paris Review,* Summer/Fall, 1986.

Stein, Leo. *Appreciations*. New York: Crown, 1947.

Steward, Samuel M.. *Dear Sammy: Letters From Gertrude Stein and Alice B. Toklas*. Boston: Houghton Mifflin Co., 1977.

This Quarter, Ethel Morehead (ed.). Paris. Spring, Summer, Fall, 1929.

Toklas, Alice B.. *The Alice B. Toklas Cook Book*. London: Michael Joseph Ltd., 1954.

Toklas, Alice B.. *What is Remembered*. San Francisco: North Point Press, 1985.

Tomkins, Calvin. *Living Well is the Best Revenge.* New York: Viking Press, 1962.

Transatlantic Review. Ford Madox Ford (ed.). Paris: 1923-1927.

transition. Eugene Jolas & Elliot Paul, (eds.). Paris: 2 (May 1927); 7 (Oct. 1927); 10 (Jan. 1928); 11 (Feb. 1928); 12 (March 1928).

Wharton, Edith. *A Backward Glance.* New York: Charles Scribner's Sons, 1964.

Whitman, George. "Rag and Bone Shop of the Heart". In *Paris Magazine,* (Autumn, 1984).

Wickes, George. *Americans in Paris.* New York: Doubleday & Co., 1969.

Williams, Roger. "Let's Meet at La Coupole." In *European Travel and Life,* New York: (December, 1987).

Williams, W. C.. *The Autobiography of William Carlos Williams.* New York: New Direction Publishing Corp, 1967.

Wilson, Edmund. *A Literary Chronicle: 1920-1950.* New York: Doubleday & Co., 1950.

Wilson, Edmund. *The Twenties.* New York: Farrar, Strauss and Giroux, 1975.

Wiser, William. *The Crazy Years: Paris in the Twenties.* New York: Atheneum, 1983.

Wolf, Geoffrey. *Black Sun.* London: Hamish Hamilton, 1947.

Wolfe, Thomas. *Of Time and the River.* New York: Charles Scribner's Sons, 1971.